RANDOM HOUSE

LARGE PRINT

ALSO BY
TIM RUSSERT

AVAILABLE FROM
RANDOM HOUSE
LARGE PRINT

Big Russ and Me

*Wisdom
of Our
Fathers*

TIM RUSSERT

Wisdom of Our Fathers

LESSONS AND LETTERS
FROM DAUGHTERS
AND SONS

RANDOM HOUSE
LARGE PRINT

Cover design: Carl D. Galian
Front-cover photograph:
© Kelly Campbell Photography
Back-cover photograph: The Buffalo News

The Library of Congress has established a
Cataloging-in-Publication record for this title.

ISBN: 978-0-7393-7752-9

www.randomhouse.com/largeprint

First Large Print Paperback Edition

Printed in the United States of America

10 9 8 7 6 5 4 3 2 1

This Large Print edition published in accord with
the standards of the N.A.V.H.

In memory of my mom,
and in honor of my dad

Contents

Introduction

In the spring of 2004, I published a book about my father—about the lessons I have learned from him, the ways he has influenced me, and my enormous love and respect for this steady, hardworking, and modest man. **Big Russ & Me** came out in May, and my publisher sent me on a publicity tour in the hope that people around the country would see the book as an ideal Father's Day gift.

Early in the tour I was in Chicago, where, to my great relief, customers were lining up to buy the book and have me autograph it. What happened next really surprised me.

"Make it out to Big Mike," somebody told me, which was followed in rapid succession by:

"This is for Big Mario."

"Please inscribe it to Big Manuel."

"For Big Irv."

"Big Willie."

"Big Stan."

I had expected that my book would appeal

to readers in my hometown of Buffalo, New York, but I didn't know whether the story of a young man coming of age in a blue-collar Irish-Catholic neighborhood, whose father was a truck driver and sanitation man, would strike a chord with a wider audience. As I soon discovered, there were many Big Russes out there—good, industrious, patriotic men who had a lot in common with my dad, even if they didn't share his religion or heritage. By writing a book about my father, I was affirming not only his life, but the lives of many other fathers as well.

"You could have been writing about **my** dad," people told me. Or, "Your dad was just like mine—a man of few words but a lot of love." Or, "Thank you for talking about your dad in such a positive way, because that was my experience too."

Here and there, somebody would hand me a note and ask me to read it when I had a free moment. Later that day, I would learn a little about that dad: his favorite saying, or the lessons he taught (sometimes by his words but more often by his actions), or the story of how hard he had worked to feed his family and educate his kids. During TV and radio interviews about the book, the hosts would begin by asking me about Big Russ but would soon describe their own dads and how much they meant to them.

I realized early on that the book was resonating far beyond what I had anticipated. Without intending to, I had given many readers an opportunity—an invitation, really—to talk about their fathers. They had listened to my story, and now I was listening to theirs.

One other bookstore moment stays with me. I was seated at a table at a Barnes & Noble on Fifth Avenue in Manhattan, where book signings are so common that the staff has developed a procedure for moving people along with great efficiency. Somebody opens the book to the title page and hands it to you along with a note, so you'll know how to spell the name of the person for whom you will inscribe it. When I read the name of Alfred Tanz, it rang a bell, although I couldn't quite remember why. Looking up, I saw a small elderly man standing in front of me.

"You don't recognize me, do you?" he asked. "I delivered your son Luke into the world."

I stood up and hugged him. "Dr. Tanz! I can't tell you what this means to me!"

"Well, I had to come. Your son was almost ten pounds!"

I hadn't recognized him without the scrubs, and also because he had seemed like a giant to me then. We hadn't seen each other since August 22, 1985, the happiest day of my life. Maureen had been going through a long and difficult labor, and at one point I left the hospital for a breath of air. Finding myself in front of a church, I went in and prayed for a healthy baby and a healthy mother. A few hours later, my prayers were answered.

I was overwhelmed to see this man again—especially here, especially now. There I was, celebrating my love for my father, and here was the man who, nineteen years earlier, had welcomed me into that very special club with seven unforgettable words: "Congratulations, Dad. You have a baby boy." Dr. Tanz was the first person to call me Dad—the best name I have ever been called.

People often say that having a child changes your life, and of course they're right, but it's hard to understand what that really means until it happens to you. In my pre-father years, I was driven, a man in a hurry. I was the first member of my family to attend college, and from there I went on to law school. I served as counsel to New York senator Daniel Patrick Moynihan, which led, eventually, to a similar position in the governor's office in Albany, which was followed by an executive job at NBC. Now I was living in Manhattan, enjoying a fast-paced life that revolved around my career. Fatherhood was the farthest thing from my mind. When I saw someone bring an infant on an airplane and stuff all that baby equipment into the overhead bin, I regarded it as an inconvenience. I would look at my watch and think, **Come on, let's get this plane in the air.**

But when Luke was born, I suddenly understood the meaning of unconditional love. I knew exactly why my father had worked two full-time jobs for thirty years and why, when I was a boy, my mother had spent her days sitting next to me when I was sick, putting her hand on my forehead to measure my fever and placing warm tea bags on my eyes to soothe the pain. My love for Luke was natural, complete, and instinctive.

Suddenly there were no more spontaneous happy hours after work, no more late-night movies, and you couldn't have paid me to attend a dinner party. My career became secondary to the blessing of being a father. I **liked** that—loved it, actually. I **wanted** to stay home to feed our baby. I **wanted** to watch him learn to crawl and say his first words. I **wanted** to coach his baseball and soccer games. I sometimes feel as if I can remember every day of my son's life.

Of course, there have been some painful moments along the way. Not long ago, when I took Luke to Boston to begin his freshman year of college, I knew as the door to his dorm room closed that a major chapter in his life— and mine too—had just come to an end. He would never again be totally dependent on me. (Actually, that had been true for years, but as long as he lived at home while in high school, I could still pretend otherwise.) Before I drove off, I gave him some simple advice: "Study hard. Laugh often. Keep your honor." I hope I've taught him to make good decisions and that I've given him a strong moral foundation to do the right thing. When my life is over, I know that the most important thing I'll be judged on is what kind of father I was.

I had hoped my book would connect with readers, but I certainly didn't anticipate how it might affect members of my own family, including the man whose name is in the title. Luke, Maureen, and I always go to Buffalo for

Thanksgiving, and in 2004, a few months after the book came out, we were loading up the car to drive to the airport when Big Russ came over to me to say good-bye. For as long as I can remember, Dad and I had always parted with a handshake and a half hug. But this time he gave me a huge bear hug and said softly, "I love you"—something I had never heard him say before. I was fifty-four years old, and all I could think was, **Boy, I wish I had written this book thirty years earlier!**

Dad needed to know it was all right to express his love to me, and my book had assured him that it was. Now that I had declared my love for him—and in public—something between us changed forever.

About a month later, Maureen, Luke, and I went back to Buffalo for Christmas Eve and then on to New York, where we attended midnight mass. When we returned to our apartment, Luke disappeared to take a shower. A few minutes later, I heard Maureen yelling, "My God, what have you done?" She ran into the room, horrified. "He has a tattoo!"

I jumped out of my chair and yelled, "Luke, come in here!" I was really mad. A few months earlier, when he had told me he wanted a tattoo, I brought up the possible health risks and pointed out the irreversibility of a youthful decision that he might someday regret. I had talked him out of it—or so I thought.

But here he was before me, with a towel around his waist and his arms firmly locked down.

"Let me see it."

"No."

"Let me see it!"

"No!"

"Luke, let me see it!"

He reluctantly raised his left arm, and there were the letters TJR. Those are my initials—and also my dad's. Luke was misty eyed. "After I read your book," he said, "I wanted you and Grandpa to always be on my side."

I collapsed back into the chair—speechless—and then sobbed. Luke came over and wrapped his arms around me. Laughing and crying at the same time, I pledged never to complain about Luke's tattoo again. I was honored to be on his side . . . forever.

In November, my dad had reacted to my book by telling me flat out that he loved me. And now, just a month later, in a very different way, so had my son. Of all the things I have done in my professional career, nothing has been more rewarding than writing that book.

. . .

I didn't think I would write another one. But when I read the letters I received from readers, I realized I had no choice.

Some of them were personal reactions. "After reading your book," one letter began, "I just knew I had to call my father." Or, "Your book about your dad has caused me to see my own dad in a different light."

Most of the letters described a father's sacrifice, fortitude, and perseverance; told of his advice and guidance; or gave examples of his kindness, generosity, love, and, yes, wisdom. Many of the letters were unforgettable. They deserved to be read—and remembered.

Early in 2005, when I decided to put together a collection of letters about other people's fathers—not a sequel, exactly, but a book that grew directly out of the response to the first one—I called Bill Novak, my editor and writing partner, and asked him to work with me again. I didn't know quite what this new book would look like, but there was one thing I was sure of—it wouldn't be limited to sons.

Growing up, I could see that my three sisters had a relationship with Big Russ that was very different from mine, and I hoped, by including stories from women, to enhance the new book and give it more depth. And how! As you'll see, the submissions from daughters tend to be more direct, open, and expressive, while the men's letters (with some exceptions) are more measured. In the end, though, both groups arrive at the same conclusion: They owe an enormous debt to their dads, and they want the world to know it.

At the same time, many of our correspondents don't **need** the world to know. As one man put it, "Whether this letter is included in your new book or not, I am grateful for the inspiration you've provided to write this piece about my dad." Or, "Even if this story about my dad isn't chosen, I want to thank you for making me finally write it down, so his great-grandchildren can read it some day and know the kind of man he was."

I received close to sixty thousand letters and e-mails, and I read them all.

The submissions included in this book address many aspects of fatherhood, but they have a few things in common. First, they are overwhelmingly positive. I knew early on that I wanted to present a favorable picture of fathers—not because all fathers are good, which obviously isn't the case, but because there has been so much talk in recent years about bad parents and dysfunctional families that I was hoping to redress the imbalance. Jennifer Kozlansky of Factoryville, Pennsylvania, brought up another reason. "It makes me cringe," she wrote, "to see how they portray fathers on TV today: stupid, incapable when it comes to caretaking, insensitive, beer-drinking, sports-obsessed, and generally clueless. Every father I know is nothing like those TV dads, and my father was the complete opposite."

Although the focus here is almost exclusively on good dads—and also because of that—it's only fair to acknowledge the occasional dissenting voice. "My dad was a beast," wrote a man in Oregon. "The one thing I learned from him was to stay out of his way. . . . I learned much more about love from my dogs than I ever did from my dad."

Most of the fathers you'll read about in this book are not superdads. They are, by and large, ordinary men with the normal distribution of human flaws and shortcomings, regular dads who try hard and sometimes succeed. What you will read here are vivid accounts of their best moments. In many cases, these fathers would be surprised, and maybe even shocked, to discover that this is what their son or daughter has remembered. But you never really know how your words or your actions will affect your children. What will they say about you when you're gone? What moment will they remember? What will they tell their children about you?

The second big theme in these letters is that the most precious things a father can provide are time, attention, and love. For about six months I read hundreds of e-mails and letters every day, but I can't recall a single one that said, "My father gave me every material thing I wanted," or, "What I remember most about my dad is the new TV he bought me." What we remember about our fathers has little or nothing to do with material objects. We remember the time they gave us—whether indirectly (through hard work) or in more conventional ways—time spent providing advice, telling a bedtime story, or simply showing up for a recital, a spelling bee, or an athletic event. There's a reason one of these chapters is called "Being There."

As I was working on this book, I came across a comment by Michael Caine, the English actor who has appeared in **Alfie, The Cider House**

Rules, and more than a hundred other movies. "My greatest conceit, and I am very conceited about it, is that I am a great father," he said. "My daughters will tell you that. I was always involved with my children. . . . I always regarded the most valuable thing I could give to my children was time." That's quite a statement, coming from a man whose busy career would leave most people with very few hours even to think about their parental responsibilities. If real estate is about location, location, location, fatherhood is about time, time, time.

It's been said a million times, but it's so true: Time is the most precious commodity of all. You can shower a child with presents or money, but what do they really mean, compared to the most valuable gift of all—your time? Your time together doesn't have to be programmed or planned. Vacations and special events are nice, but so often the best moments are the spontaneous ones, when nothing much is happening. You can't create those moments, but you can encourage them, and the way to do that is simply by being there. Every moment you spend with your child could be the one that really matters. End of sermon.

The third theme I noticed was that many of the fathers you'll read about are relatively silent and modest men. As I worked on this book, I read many war stories, which often depicted moments of bravery and great courage. But with remarkable frequency, even with stories about heroism, the son or the daughter recounting these events pointed out that their father spoke about them rarely—and sometimes not at all.

For the most part, the fathers in this book are not big talkers, and although their daughters and sons understand that this is, in part, a generational difference, there are times when a more expressive generation finds their fathers' silence frustrating. By the same token, most of these fathers are not inclined to brag. They don't take up much space in the world, but their impact on their children has been profound. "My dad wasn't anyone special," I heard time and time again, "but he sure was special to me."

The fourth theme, which is related to the third one, is that sons and daughters who were born during and after the postwar baby boom are often acutely aware of how their fathers never said the words **I love you**—or said them only after an unexpected intervention, following years of being emotionally unexpressive. Some daughters and sons find these missing declarations of love to be painful, while others take it in stride. "My father never told us that he loved us," somebody wrote, "but he never had to. It was clear in everything he did."

Several people described the moment when everything changed. One young man had never heard his father express his love until the night before he left for basic training, when his dad gave him a watch and said, "I love you, son." Another correspondent remembers when her father, in his seventies, broke into tears while talking about his own father. He told her that the biggest regret of his life was that he hadn't told his father how much he loved him before he died. "As **my** father grew old," she writes, "I told him all the time how much I loved him. When he died, I felt at peace because I had expressed my love."

For Alan Thompson of Albany, Georgia, the turning point came while he was in the hospital for an operation. His father phoned when Alan was still groggy from anesthesia, and in his uninhibited state the patient blurted out, "I love you, Dad," which he hadn't said since elementary school. There was a pregnant silence on the line. Then, for the first time in Alan's memory, his father said, "I love you, lad. Hang in there." From then on, he writes, "Every time we had the chance to be together, he'd pour a couple of scotch and waters and we'd talk, man to man, about the good old days, about cars, women, and the military, and all the things I had always wished he would talk to me about. We knew we loved each other. We didn't have to say it, but we said it anyway."

Madeline Labriola, a retired teacher in upstate New York, had never felt close to her father, who seemed distant and unapproachable. When she went off to college, she was enormously homesick. One night, feeling despondent, she called home and her father answered. She doesn't remember what they talked about, but at the end of the conversation, she surprised herself by blurting out, "Dad, I love you!"

"From that moment," she writes, "our relationship changed. Those three little words pulled aside the curtain that had kept me from seeing my father for what he truly was— my protector, my provider, my cheerleader, my hero."

There are many lessons in this book, and this, surely, is one of them: **If you are a father, let your kids know, in plain English, that you love them.** Yes, I know, it's always implied, but even so, it's a wonderful thing to hear—and to say. And if you are fortunate enough to have a father and he has never said those words, he may just need a little encouragement.

It works in the other direction as well. One of the earliest letters I received came from Roger Howard, a real estate agent in Indianapolis. A few years ago, his son, John, had planned to drive alone from Indianapolis to the West Coast after graduating from college. As the start of the trip approached, John began to understand the magnitude of the undertaking—the time, the distance, the unfamiliar roads, and (no small matter) the expense—and asked if his father could take three weeks and join him. As Roger put it, "Saying yes was one of the easiest and fastest decisions I've ever made."

At the end of three wonderful weeks, John dropped his father at the San Francisco airport for his flight home. With time to kill before takeoff, Roger opened his shaving kit, where he found a note that John had written the night before, while his father slept, in which he told his father how important the trip and their relationship were. "Long story short," writes Roger, "I sat there in the middle of the airport, bawling my eyes out."

Roger went on to offer a suggestion to me and other fathers. "Pick a destination somewhere in this country, and don't fly," he wrote. "Drive there together. Camp some along the way. Find a great restaurant in each city you drive through and go in without a tie. Buy sandwiches and sodas for a cooler and eat at interstate rest areas or along state highways. Stop at local diners. Find a ballpark, whether it's the major leagues, Little League, or the American Legion—and spend your evenings outdoors. Visit with the people you meet. You get the idea."

I did get the idea, and I even took Roger's advice, although it was a shorter trip in our case, and I compromised it to some extent by doing a few radio interviews during the drive, until Luke threatened to stop the truck unless I turned off the cell phone.

The fifth theme I noticed is that most of our correspondents are themselves fathers and mothers. That makes sense, when you think about it. A number of our contributors mentioned that it took them until adulthood—and sometimes well **into** adulthood—to fully appreciate what their fathers had given them or how he had shaped them. More than one of our correspondents quoted or alluded to Mark Twain's famous observation: "When I was a boy of fourteen, my father was so ignorant I could hardly stand to have the old man around. But when I got to be twenty-one, I was astonished at how much the old man had learned in seven years." The quote may be apocryphal—there is some doubt as to whether Twain actually wrote it—but the line still resonates.

I am enormously grateful to the many people who took the time and made the effort to send me a letter about their father. If yours was one of the overwhelming majority of submissions that I wasn't able to include, I am truly sorry. There were so many wonderful stories that this book could easily have been issued as a multivolume set.

There is one contribution in particular that I want to mention. H. J. "Dutch" Bialke, who died in 2005, was a credit analyst in the small town of Park Rapids, Minnesota, about two hundred miles north of Minneapolis, where he and his wife raised eight children who adored their father. In 2001, on the occasion of his seventy-fifth birthday, his children put together a booklet in which each of them listed seventy-five reasons why they loved him.

Barbara Bishop, a civil engineer in South Bend, Indiana, and one of Dutch Bialke's children, told me that this was the best gift their father had ever received, and when I read it I could see why. Since then, she says, she has passed this concept on to other families, who have come up with one hundred reasons as a Valentine's Day gift, fifty reasons for a golden wedding anniversary, and similar variations for notable birthdays, Mother's Days, and Father's Days. I can't imagine a more meaningful gift.

I think of this book as a kind of full-voiced choir, a chorus of voices coming together from around the country, expressing their deep and well-deserved gratitude to the first man they ever really knew. For many years, fathers who have said or done things that may not always have made sense to their children have found themselves saying, or thinking, just as **their** fathers had, "Someday you'll thank me." For most of the fathers whose sons and daughters wrote the stories you are about to read, that day is finally here.

*Wisdom
of Our
Fathers*

Small Moments

"In the years when my parents were broke, Dad would give Mom a daisy for each year they were married."
—Donna Pizzolongo, daughter of George E. Raboni Sr.

Small moments? It's often those little gestures—a knowing look, a pat on the back, an unexpected kindness—that make a big impression and shape our favorite memories. When I came home from college to visit, by the time I woke up in the morning Big Russ had already cleaned my car inside and out (windows too) and filled up the gas tank. I once realized too late that I had left behind evidence of a spirited evening the night before, but Dad was nice enough not to mention it.

Dad's small moments weren't limited to me. When one of my sisters had a hard time, especially after breaking up with a boyfriend, Mom would console her, of course, but Dad would be there too, trying to change the subject—often with some good humor. He didn't always know how to comfort his daughters, but he always tried, and they appreciated his efforts.

As a new father, I looked forward to providing some small moments for my son, and I hope there have been many. I have also been on the receiving end of quite a few, and they started very early. When Luke was two, I went to China with the **Today** show. My wife, Maureen, flew over to join me for the final week, leaving Luke with her mother and sister in San Francisco. It was difficult for us to be away from him for so long, and on the flight home I actually found myself wondering if our little boy would remember us. When the plane landed in California, we went through customs, picked up our luggage, and looked up to the glass-enclosed balcony where family and friends were waiting to greet the passengers. And there, next to his grandmother, was our little Luke, jumping up and down with excitement. My heart pounded. It was one of the most beautiful sights I have ever seen.

Flash forward about sixteen years. When Luke was graduating from high school, his class asked me to give the commencement address. It was a great honor, but this was the most difficult speech of my life: I had to say something meaningful and inspiring without in any way embarrassing my son. I spoke from the heart and gave the class a kind of blessing: "May you always love your own children as much as your parents love you, as much as

Maureen and I love our Luke." I must have passed the test, because when I finished speaking, the class rose to its feet in appreciation—led by Luke.

Then, one by one, the students came up to receive their diplomas. When it was Luke's turn, the headmaster motioned for me to take over for a moment. Neither Luke nor I had been prepared for this possibility, and again I wondered how he would react. To my delight, when I gave him the diploma, I received a rib-crushing bear hug from my six-foot-two baby boy. I actually had to say, "Luke, enough. Put me down!" His classmates laughed. It was funny, but there was more in that embrace than humor.

The graduating seniors received their yearbooks that day, and each student had been given a full page to reflect on his high school career. That night, when I got into bed, I began flipping through Luke's copy. His page began with expressions of gratitude. "Dad," said the first one, "you're the driving force behind it all, and my best friend in the world. Thanks for always having my back. I love you."

Now if you had asked me to identify a specific moment when I had Luke's back, I couldn't point to one. He was reminding me that tender moments are the ultimate wisdom—whether it's the mutual love and respect that two parents share, a supportive word, or one of the many little comments and gestures of daily life that are more powerful than any lecture. Small moments accumulate and last a lifetime and, what's more, they get carried on into the next generation.

I lay back, smiled, and closed my misty eyes. The pillow had never seemed so soft.

THE SOLDIER

A father who wipes away twenty years with a single hug.

One thing I'll never forget about my father—a hard-as-nails tough-love man who fought in two world wars and a war in Africa during the twenties—was the single tear running down his cheek the day he dropped me off at Fort Dix on my way to Vietnam, and the one hug that made up for twenty-two years of no hugging. Only he could understand what the coming year had in store for me. He couldn't even share his sorrow with my mother. Because of her weak heart, we told her I was going to a missile base in Guam. It seemed as if all the years of absence from each other's lives came together at that moment in New Jersey. We finally shared a bond no one else in my family could ever understand, father to son, man to man, soldier to soldier.

—Joseph E. Colussi, Spring Grove, PA,
retired telephone tech, son of Peter C.
Colussi, mosaic artist (1900–1975)

THE TOUCH

It was a routine gesture during an ordinary car ride, but she still remembers it.

As a young child, I sometimes stuttered. Once, when I was six and our family was traveling in the car, I was trying to tell my parents something and couldn't get the words out. Stuttering confused me, which caused me to stutter even more. Although this didn't happen very often, it was painful for my parents to witness. That day, while my dad was driving, he calmly reached into the backseat and pulled me closer to him. Then he put his arm around my shoulders and patted my right arm. I remember feeling a sense of immediate calm that allowed me to get the words out.

—Kerry A. Bostwick,
Mount Vernon, IA, associate professor,
daughter of Robert R. Bostwick,
superintendent of schools (1927)

THE SAME ROOM

Father Theodore Hesburgh, longtime president of the University of Notre Dame, said it best: "The most important thing a father can do for his children is to love their mother."

I was visiting my parents a few years after my mother's health started failing, when my dad had completely taken over her care and the house. I was up early and heard them talking. I didn't want to disturb the moment, and I tried not to listen, but I overheard my mother tell Dad that she was sorry she was such a poor companion these days. She wanted to be traveling and doing things together, as they had often discussed.

There was silence, and then Dad said, in a choked voice, "Don't you know I just want to be in the same room with you?" I was struck by the simplicity and love in that remark, as my mother was a complex and brilliant woman given to philosophy. I loved my parents for the example of their relationship.

My mother died several years ago. Dad is still alive, but he is suffering from some dementia. He lives with me now, and I have come to understand the simplicity and importance of being in the same room with him.

—**KATHERINE M. NEWBOLD, Peru, IL, FBI (retired), daughter of John M. Newbold, FBI, state police (1920)**

THE LOCK

There is nothing like something that's just between you and your dad.

My father was a talented man who liked to build things in his fully equipped workshop in our basement. My little brother liked to follow him downstairs to watch and "help" as Dad made such things as chandeliers from old wagon wheels, a rotisserie for our fireplace, and an unusual light fixture out of the copper bulbs that float in the tank of a toilet.

When Jim was seven, he began going to Dad's workshop on his own, where he would remove Dad's tools from their rightful place, use them, and not replace them. After telling him many times about the importance of putting things back, Dad decided to build a small tool chest with a lock, where he would keep his best tools so my brother couldn't get at them.

As Dad worked on the tool chest, my brother watched him and helped enthusiastically. As Dad was installing the lock, Jim asked, "What's that?" Dad said it was a lock, and that in order to get tools from the chest, you had to open it with a key. Jim got a strange look on his face. He looked up at his father and asked, "Who will have the key, Dad?"

Dad paused a moment, reflected on the look on his son's face, and said, "There will be just two keys, Jim. One for you and one for me."

—MERABETH LURIE, Hubbard, OH, retired teacher, daughter of Jerold S. Meyer, retail executive (1903–1997)

THE ANNOUNCEMENT

It was a tough thing to hear, and an even tougher thing to say, but within a day they were right back on track.

Coming out to my dad was one of the most difficult experiences of my life, as it is for most young gay men. After all, our dads represent

all things masculine, strong, and "normal"—
words not commonly associated with the gay
community.

My announcement was not exactly a text-
book example of how it should be done.
Note to closeted gays: Don't tell your dad
during the ten o'clock news, right before he's
going to bed.

Despite my poor timing, my dad responded
as many dads do. He cried all night. The next
morning, he watched me pass in the living
room, my head and shoulders slung low and
my eyes focused on the floor beneath me. I
was feeling the utter shame of the grave disappointment I had caused him.

By the fourth time our paths crossed, he had
seen enough. He grabbed my shoulders, pulled
them back, and said, "Look me in the eye." I
refused. Again he said, "Stephen, look me in
the eye." This time I did. With tears rolling
down his face, he looked right at me and said,
"I love you, Stephen. I don't care what you are.
I just want my boys to be happy." Then he
hugged me, just like he did the day before,
when I was straight.

That's all I ever wanted and needed—to
know I would still be loved. Five years later, my
relationship with my dad has never been

stronger. We still talk daily after each Cubs game. I still ask for advice with my job. And my dad still asks if I'm dating anyone, although this time around he wants to know if I've met any good guys lately.

Unconditional love. That's all we ever want, and I got it.

—STEPHEN WESTMAN, Chicago, IL,
vibe manager, son of Gary Westman,
sales (1945)

THE GRADUATE

Just because a dad doesn't show his emotions doesn't mean he isn't full of feelings.

My father was the strong, silent type who wasn't effusive or openly affectionate.

I was the first one in our family to graduate from college. Two weeks before graduation, we were having a normal family dinner when out of the clear blue, my father broke into uncontrollable sobbing. He left the table, followed by my mother. A few minutes later she came back with tears in her own eyes. She explained that my father was overcome by the emotion of my imminent graduation from college, and that if it hadn't been for the Depression and the war, this was what he had hoped to do at my age. Never again did I see such emotion from him, and that included my wedding and the adoption of my only son. He passed away more than twenty years ago, but each spring, with the arrival of graduation season, I think back to the day when I learned how proud strong, silent Stan was of his oldest son.

—DAVID S. WROBEL, Syracuse, NY,
retired, son of Stanley J. Wrobel,
machinist (1918–1983)

THE BREAKUP

Time is not the only thing that heals. So do kind words.

When one of my silly boyfriends and I broke up and I thought I was heartbroken, my whole family tried to cheer me up. When everyone else had gone off to bed, my father turned back to me and said, "You know, I love you so much that I'd marry you if I could." That was the nicest thing anyone had ever said to me, and I was speechless. I don't think I even said good night.

—JEAN A. ASTORINO, Media, PA,
optometrist, daughter of Ross Astorino,
equipment operator (1922–2001)

THE SHAVE

Who ever imagined that the memory of learning to shave with Dad could turn a man's life around?

A few years ago, I became the victim of a senseless, unprovoked act of violence that left several scars on my neck. I survived, and the assailant is in prison, but I will never really be the same. When I shave I see one of the scars, and, until recently, to see that scar was to trigger a visual memory of my assailant's rage-filled face.

The obvious solution was to stop shaving, but that didn't work. I began to remember the terrible event with increasing vividness, until I finally sought help.

My therapist's first question to me was, "Do you have a good relationship with your father?"

I said, "Yes. We have a great relationship."

The therapist asked if he had taught me how to shave. Before I could answer, a memory I had forgotten for many, many years popped into my head, and I smiled.

"Doctor," I replied, "this is so cool. I remember standing at my dad's side as a little boy, infatuated with the process of shaving. It got to the point that when he shaved in the mornings I was always there, watching him. My dad bought me a little toy razor, with a little knob on the bottom of the handle that opened the top, just like his. The blade was a piece of cardboard that looked like a razor blade.

"After that, I got to smear shaving cream all over my face and shave with my dad."

My therapist then suggested that I think of this happier memory every time I shaved, to displace the memory of the attack.

And, indeed, the "new" memory has replaced the violent one. Now, when I shave, I feel the love my dad showed me, and I also remember what it felt like to be innocent. My shaving memory marked the start of a long journey best described as posttraumatic growth.

Precious memories are made in an instant

and last forever. I am so thankful that my dad had the patience back then to let me "shave." That memory has strengthened an already strong relationship, and what made me happy then is making me a happier man today. Bless you, Dad.

—MARK BRENNAMAN,
Oklahoma City, OK, quit-smoking coach,
son of Ernest Brennaman,
oil company executive (1925)

THE DAISIES

He really loved her mother—and she's still grateful for that.

In the years when my parents were broke, Dad would give Mom a daisy for each year they were married. In the good years he would send her a rose for each year of married life. On the night before their twenty-fifth anniversary, twenty-five daisies arrived with a card that said, **Come take my hand. . . .** The next morning, on their actual anniversary, twenty-five roses arrived, with a card that said, **Grow old along with me. . . .** Then he gave her a silver bell (Mom collected bells), and on it was engraved, **The best is yet to be. Love, G.** When Dad died, Mom had THE BEST IS YET TO BE carved on his headstone.

—DONNA PIZZOLONGO, Columbia, SC,
mortgage underwriter, daughter of
George E. Raboni Sr., attorney (1933–1985)

THE KISS

You are never too old for a father's love.

My dad loved the fact that he had two daughters, and although we were by no means wealthy, he spoiled us as much as he could. He was a tailor who came over from Italy as a boy. He went back once, with his mother, and returned at sixteen, having already learned a craft. He and my mother worked hard each day in their little cleaning and tailor shop. He never said no to me and never yelled at me, even when he should have.

When my husband was in Vietnam and I was pregnant, he would come into my room in the morning with a cup of coffee for me, and he would come in again at night and kiss me. I always pretended to be sleeping. He had done this when I was a child, and he continued to do it as long as I was in his house.

There are a lot of great fathers out there, but mine could be tender without saying a word.

—JOANNE EVANGELISTA,
Farmington Hills, MI, wife, mother,
daughter of Sam Poolello, tailor
(1921–1974)

THE WATERMELON

Her dad created a brief moment of magic. She enjoyed it then, and she still enjoys it now.

On a warm summer evening in western New York when I was seven, my dad and I were eating watermelon slices on what we called our patio: We would open the garage door, place lawn chairs at the top of the driveway, and watch the neighborhood.

My brother always swallowed the watermelon seeds, but I saved mine in a pile on the edge of the plate. "Do you think if I plant these in the ground a watermelon will grow?"

I asked my dad. "Sure!" he replied. "In fact, if you plant Cheerios in the ground, you can grow donuts, too!"

With this exciting horticultural project in mind, I took my pile of small, slippery seeds and placed them on a paper towel to dry overnight. I was eager to plant them the next morning.

The next day was Saturday. My dad popped his head through the side door of the garage as I was digging six small holes in the soil along the strip of land we shared with our next-door neighbors. "Are you going to grow that watermelon?" he asked.

"Sure am!" I replied as I patted the dirt on top of the six neat crevices. It was only 8:30 A.M., so the watermelon had the entire day to emerge.

An hour later, I ran to where I planted the seeds to see if the watermelon had grown. Believe it or not, there was not even a sprout. An hour later I checked again. Still nothing. While I was eating lunch, my dad was standing outside the house and called to me, "Mary Jo! Come here!" I ran outside so fast I broke the sound barrier.

"What is it?" I asked.

"I just wanted to let you know that the watermelon hasn't grown yet." He pulled this stunt over and over, until I finally started to ignore him when he called me.

After a few days, I put the watermelon plant out of my mind and continued with the other important issues of being seven, when suddenly my mother called me from my bedroom. "Mary Jo! Come outside!" I went out the front door and followed her calls to the side of the house. Right there, vertically positioned, stood a perfect green watermelon that had apparently grown directly from the ground. My dad stood next to her, feigning amazement at my green thumb. "It's incredible! We'll have a party!"

Later that evening, several of the neighbors came over to our "patio." We cracked open the watermelon, and Dad made it known that I was a superstar for growing this amazing fruit. I was too excited and too naïve to notice that the price tag was still on it.

—**MARY JO FERRO**, **East Amherst, NY,**
sales rep, daughter of Charles E. Darling,
industrial sales (1934–2005)

Daddy's Girl

"I was an only child. Mom said I was plenty; Dad said I was perfect."
—BETH HACKETT, daughter of Roger Hackett

I've often heard it said that girls are harder to raise than boys, especially during adolescence. Although I can't speak from direct experience, from what I've seen I'm inclined to believe it. Certainly girls are **different,** especially for fathers.

I have never seen my dad happier than on the day my older sister got married. He was pleased and proud of both B.A. and her husband—and, also, by the way, of the roast beef at the end of the buffet table at the reception. ("I'm telling you, it's beautiful.") When I saw him dancing with the new bride with a real bounce in his step, it was the first time that I really saw my father as a younger man. It's a powerful scene in my mind, and as I selected the letters for this section, that image kept coming back to me: Dad dancing with his daughter. To me, that's what it means to be a daddy's girl.

I've had many advantages and privileges in my life that my dad never had the opportunity to enjoy, but I've never had a daughter. Some of the toughest kids I knew in high school and college talk with pride about their daughters and will often say, "She has me wrapped around her finger." But there's no regret in that statement—just love and, strangely enough, a measure of pride too.

When I asked Maria Shriver about her father, Sargent Shriver, founder of the Peace Corps and George McGovern's running mate in 1972, she said that when she was first going out with Arnold Schwarzenegger, Arnold offered to send her a plane ticket so she could visit him in California. Hearing that, her father sent her a long letter. "Do not accept an airline ticket from a man," he wrote, "because you will owe him. And don't ever put yourself in a position where you owe anything about yourself to a man"—she was surprised to read her father's words, as he continued—"because I know what a man thinks he's going to get for an airline ticket." No matter who you are, a dad is still a dad.

When women are pleased with their fathers, it's often because of their fathers' guidance and protection. And when they're disappointed in their fathers, it's often for the same reason they are disappointed in their boyfriends and their husbands—most men just aren't very expressive. In 1981, Jane Fonda had the unusual experience of making a movie with her father. **On Golden Pond** was a case of art imitating life, with Henry Fonda playing the taciturn father, and Jane playing the daughter who wanted them to be closer. "A lot of Norman Thayer was my father," she told me. "He had a hard time expressing emotions. I think that's why the movie meant so much to so many people, because many of us have had fathers like that."

Then she told me about a fascinating moment in the movie. "Dad didn't like to have anything happen that hadn't been rehearsed. It really bothered him. And I **wanted** to do something that hadn't been rehearsed, because I wanted to see emotion rise in him. And so in the last close-up on him, when I said, 'I want to be your friend,' I reached out and I touched his arm, and I could see on his face; it just took him—I mean, it's microscopic, but it took him, and the tears came immediately, and he ducked his head like this because he didn't want anyone to see, but I saw. I saw."

That moment meant so much to her. When the day's shooting was done, she asked her father if she could come to his house for dinner. She was hoping to build on that earlier moment and to see whether the chemistry between them had changed as a result of that scene. To her disappointment, it hadn't—or at least not that her father would admit to.

And yet she felt blessed to have made a movie with her dad and to have their relationship grow—at least on film—for at the end of the movie he put his arm around her and they embraced.

Henry Fonda won his only Oscar for **On Golden Pond;** he died five months later. His daughter's lasting memory of him was that spontaneous moment in their movie, but when she asked him to reinforce it with his words, he couldn't. "Couldn't do it, no," she said, "but maybe he wanted to." Is it ever too late to be a daddy's girl? Hope lives on.

THE DOLL

A father's presence can extend well beyond the course of his life.

My father developed rheumatic fever as a baby, which left him with a damaged heart. His illness came back periodically, and he had to go to the hospital. But he never allowed his medical problems to interfere with his life. He loved my sister and me more than anything, and he often told us so.

When I was ten, I was given a Kewpie doll for Christmas, which became my favorite doll. My dad and I decided to call him Butchie. Dad worked second shift as an electrician, so when I started going to school, I didn't see him much during the week; he was gone before I got home, and he returned after I went to bed. Most days, when I got home from school, Butchie would be doing something special, like sliding down the banister, playing outside in the dirt, or sitting at the table eating a cookie. One afternoon I came home and found Butchie in my bed with the measles. My dad had drawn red spots all over his face, and because they didn't wash off, Butchie was destined to spend the rest of his days that way.

When I graduated from high school, I got a secretarial job. After I had worked a year, the company where I worked offered a bus trip to New York City and I decided to go—the first time I had ever gone out of town without a member of my family. I was eighteen at the time, and when I got to the hotel room and my roommates and I were opening our suitcases, I saw that, on top of everything else, there was Butchie with his trademark smile and the red spots on his face.

Two years later, when I got married, Dad walked me down the aisle with tears in his eyes. I felt a little sad—I was no longer his little girl—but when we arrived at our honeymoon destination, I began unpacking and there was Butchie to remind me: No matter how old I was, I would always be Daddy's little girl.

—RUTH KELLY, Hinsdale, MA,
retired benefits specialist,
daughter of Milton Sherman,
electrician (1908–1973)

THE COMPANION

Finding meaning and even joy in a simple, routine, and daily activity—what a blessing!

Have you ever thought about why you do some of the things you do? Is it all simple routine or does it have meaning? Your morning cup of coffee, for example. Do you drink it for the taste or because you need a jolt? For me it's neither.

Don't get me wrong, I love coffee. The smell of freshly ground beans, the silky sweet taste, the warmth of the mug in my hands—these are good reasons to drink coffee, but I drink it because of my dad.

I was an only child. Mom said I was plenty; Dad said I was perfect. He worked hard to support us: twelve-hour shifts with thirteen days on and only one day off, because overtime paid the bills. He left early in the morning, long before Mom and I were awake; he came home exhausted and slept until it was time to do it all over again. It was hard on him because he had so little time with us. It was hard on us too.

We all found little ways to compensate.

Mom would pack his lunch and take one bite of his sandwich, so he would smile when it was time to eat. I would put my favorite toy in his lunch box so he had something to play with at work.

Dad's special time for me was morning coffee. He would get up at 4 A.M., start the coffee brewing, and get ready for work. When the pot was ready, he would come into my room and wake me up. I would sit at the kitchen table as he poured two cups of coffee. His was always black. Mine was barely brown, full of milk and sugar, sweet to the taste. Dad would tell me about his day and ask about mine. When the cups were empty, he would tuck me back into bed and kiss me good night before heading out to work. It was our special time together, and we never missed.

When I moved away from home, we talked on the phone every day. Now our special time was cooking dinner together. He cooked for Mom; I cooked for my husband. We never missed.

He died in 1995, and I still miss him. Every morning I make a pot of coffee and sit at the kitchen table. My coffee is still just barely brown, full of milk and sugar, sweet to the taste. When I raise my mug to my lips and drink that first sweet sip, I see my dad sitting across from me, a smile on his face and a cup of coffee in his hands. Saying good-bye does not torment me, because I know Dad will be back tomorrow. My cup of coffee is never routine. It's always special. I'm having coffee with my dad.

—BETH HACKETT, Conesus, NY, student,daughter of Roger Hackett, instrument technician (1924–1995)

THE SEND-OFF

His daughters had a special relationship with their dad, and they maintained it right to the end.

My parents had eight kids: two boys, followed by six girls. Often, after dinner, Dad would allow us girls to do whatever we wanted with him—comb his hair, put it in curlers, or paint his toenails. He was like a real live doll for us to play with. He didn't mind; sometimes he even fell asleep during his beauty treatments.

Every summer his company had a picnic. One year, when it was time to go swimming, we begged Dad to get into the pool with us. As he took off his shoes and socks, his co-workers couldn't help but notice that Dad's toenails were painted a bright shade of pink. He just laughed and said, "Those darn girls." I'm sure he didn't care who saw it, and he didn't bother to offer a fuller explanation.

This happened almost forty years ago. About ten years ago, Dad became very sick and had to go into the hospital. We agreed to take him off life support, and we arranged for it to happen when we had all arrived at his bedside. As the priest was giving him his last rites, we six girls decided that it would be fitting for Dad to enter heaven with his toenails painted. Each of us painted a toe, and amid the tears, we all burst out laughing. The hospital staff must have thought we were crazy, but we knew something they didn't: Dad would have loved it.

—DEBBIE MOORE, Dallas, TX,
administrative assistant,
daughter of Deryck Lawson,
insurance executive (1926–1996)

THE BOND

This very sweet story is from my son's freshman writing teacher at Boston College. My dad wore Aqua Velva too. I guess there is something about an Aqua Velva man.

They say there's a special bond between Italian dads and their daughters, but for me, an only child, **bond** doesn't do it justice. I worshiped the man.

Growing up, I didn't see much of him. He worked rotating shifts as an aircraft mechanic: 7 to 3, 3 to 11, and sometimes the overnight shift, 11 to 7. And with the three-to four-hour round-trip commute between Methuen, Massachusetts, and Portsmouth, New Hampshire—he went the long way to avoid the tolls—he was away from home quite a bit. My mom and I missed him on a number of holidays, and I missed having a nine-to-five dad like the rest of the kids in our neighborhood.

I remember two things most of all. First, he always saved up enough money and vacation days to take my mom and me to Seabrook Beach in New Hampshire for two weeks each summer. I was so thrilled to spend time with my dad that I'd wake him up at five every morning to start the day and go walking in the tide pools. Can you imagine being awakened by your six-year-old every day during your vacation?

He'd wake up, shave, put on Aqua Velva—the smell still reminds me of him, and it was my Christmas gift to him each year—and we'd go for a two- or three-hour walk, talking about everything from hermit crabs to choosing friends. I was always so proud to walk with my dad.

The second thing I remember are the notes he would leave me. On the nights when he was working and didn't see me, he'd sneak a note into my lunch box or schoolbag, usually on a napkin with a silly drawing on it. He'd tell me he was proud of me for learning my multiplication tables, or he'd remind me to dress warmly. I saved all those notes.

He died in 1993 of lung cancer. He was the cleanest-living man you'd ever want to meet, but the disease hit a lot of men who chose his line of work. In those days they worked without protective masks and inhaled noxious fumes.

Not long ago I was rummaging in the

garage, which is still more or less preserved as a shrine to my dad. I pulled on his heavy leather gloves, which are still too big for me and still smell faintly of Aqua Velva in the palms, over a pair of wool gloves and went looking for a can of WD-40 to lube the lopping shears that I needed for spring cleanup. As I was looking through meticulously neat cabinets and boxes, in a drawer above his toolbox I found a note. On a slightly worn paper napkin under the WD-40 and a pair of safety glasses was a drawing of a duck wearing a sombrero and poking itself accidentally with the branch of a tree. (Ducks were a popular motif in the drawings he left for me.) The note read:

Ay! Señorita Quackita, wear eye protection, beautiful brown eyes.

—Señor D.

I didn't know whether to laugh at the drawing or cry over the fact that Dad was still looking out for me. I did a little of both.

—Andrea DeFusco, Methuen, MA, college administrator, daughter of Alfred DeFusco, aircraft mechanic (1922–1993)

THE LAWYER

Her dad was gone, but one of his lessons came back to her just when she needed it.

I was raised by a wonderful, quiet, competent, and competitive man who, along with my mom, created a home of love and fun and discipline, leading my brother and me to believe we could do anything. My father spent the first part of his life on the professional tennis circuit, which was not at all lucrative back then. With a wife and two children, he said he "needed to grow up," so he gave tennis lessons at a local club in the mornings, attended law school in the afternoons, worked the loading docks of Miami International Airport at night, and played tournaments on the weekends for the little money it provided while my mom held the home front together. After law school he practiced law (with his father) and later became a judge before returning to the private sector, where he earned great respect as a litigator.

He and I were close. He coached me in tennis, in basketball, in track, and in life, and he attended every meet, game, performance, and tournament I ever had.

When I finally figured out what I wanted to do in life, it was to practice law with my dad. By then I had done every other job in the firm. I was a receptionist at twelve, when the regulars were on vacation, and had worked as janitor, filing clerk, process server, secretary, and, eventually, legal assistant.

Before I was admitted to the Florida bar, my dad was diagnosed with cancer, and he died three months after my admission. During the last two years of his life, I worked at his side, watching and learning all I could so I would be able to carry on the practice no matter what.

Within a month of Dad's death, I had my first trial. I had never even taken a deposition by myself, and in the freshness of grief I was faced with the task of proving that our client's stroke was work related. I was opposed by one of the older defense firms in Miami, but because of the man Dad was, several of his colleagues spent hours with me, strategizing, rehearsing, and teaching me tricks of the trade. When the day arrived, I sat at the claimant's table with my secretary, across from three men in three-piece suits. (One of them knew close to nothing about the case; he was there to help with intimidation.)

The trial lasted three days, and I sensed I was doing well. Opposing counsel stood for his closing statement and began, "First let me say that Al Harum's death was a huge loss for Miami's legal community." A lump jammed in the base of my throat, and it grew as he continued with expressions of how much he admired my dad. My heart began to pound and my eyes singed with that first hint of tearing.

He kept on like this until I just about lost it, but then, clear as a bell, I heard my father's voice: **Don't fall for that BS, Dolly.** My eyes dried instantly, and I looked around to see if anyone else heard it. No, just me. Suddenly I was making my closing statement, which began, "I'm glad that Mr. Herman has fond memories of my dad, but that's completely irrelevant to the case at bar." As I went on with a summation, I saw the judge nodding in agreement. We won that case, and our client's life is better because of the team of Harum and Harum.

—**ANDREA HARUM SCHIAVONI,
Sag Harbor, NY, attorney,
daughter of Al Harum Jr.,
attorney (1935–1997)**

THE RINGS

A beautiful letter from a daughter to her dad—and another reminder that it's the little things that matter most.

My father was in the Battle of the Bulge, where he experienced much sorrow. But that only made him more determined to be happy, enjoy his life, and be kind to everyone. I wrote this letter the Christmas after I lost him, when my heart ached to talk to him.

Dear Dad,

I am writing this letter to tell you how much I miss you, and to let you know that I think of you every day. I know you were old, and everybody tells me you lived longer than most people, but to me you were always just my dad and not an old person.

I remember now, as an adult, some precious memories of my childhood—not what you bought me but what you did with me.

How, when you smoked cigars, I patiently waited for you to unwrap the paper ring to wear on my finger.

How you tightened my roller skates with my skate key before I went on my journey with my friends.

How we sat together on Saturday nights, eating hot dogs and beans and watching **The Lone Ranger.**

How you sometimes gave me a quarter so I could buy a three-pack of comic books to read on a Saturday afternoon, and how you saved one of your old coffee cans just for me, to keep my marbles in.

How you praised me for my diligent hard work making pot holders and ash-trays for everyone in the family, whether they needed them or not.

How you carted Girl Scout cookies to work so I could sell the most cookies in my unit.

How you sat with me in the kitchen and tried to help with my math home-work, raising your voice only when it came to keeping my numbers in line.

How, when you polished your shoes for work the next day, you would take my shoes and shine them too.

How you would occasionally take my cousin and me for a day trip and say that whoever was the quietest in the car would get a nickel, and how I always won when you grabbed my cousin's knee and made him laugh.

How we never went to Disneyland, but it was as if I went there every summer night, when you would take my friends and me for chocolate-chip ice cream. Sometimes you would serenade us with "Racing with the Moon," by Vaughn Monroe, and I thought your singing was very good. Sometimes on the return trip we would hear "I'm Forever Blowing Bubbles" or "I'll Be Down to Get You in a Taxi, Honey." It was always those three songs, and you would always tell us the same joke. "Did you hear there was a holdup down the street?" And I would say, "Where?" And you would say, "Mrs. O'Brien held up a pair of pants with a clothespin," and I fell for it every time.

How on Saturdays you would get your haircut, and I would sit on the red leather chair waiting for you, and then we would drive to the gas station for a check on your car and the weekly chat with the gas station owner. I thought this was the best way to spend an afternoon.

And how at Christmastime you would

set up the card table and you'd show me how to wrap presents. I thought you were so smart to make the corners of the paper fold just right so the presents were all neatly wrapped.

Dad, when you got sick, I asked you if this was worse than the war, and you said it was different. My life is different now. You are gone, and I now wear Mom's diamond wedding ring that you gave me. But I am not any happier than when I wore your cigar rings and listened to you sing.

Love, Janet

—JANET SILVANO, Medford, MA,
staff assistant, daughter of
Thomas Joseph O'Brien,
corporate treasurer (1912–1999)

THE SHOES

I was surprised by how often polio was mentioned in the letters I received. For one special night back in 1962, a little girl was able to live her dream.

My father left school at sixteen, lied about his age, and joined the Marine Corps, where he survived Pearl Harbor and hitting the beaches in the Pacific. Later, he became a golf pro in Guam, where I was born in 1956. I had polio, so I wore a leg brace day and night for years and wasn't allowed to wear regular shoes.

One night when I was six, and my dad and I were out for a walk in San Francisco—we had moved there because of my need for special care—I spied a pair of Mary Jane black patent-leather shoes. I had never owned normal shoes, and Dad was between jobs, but he bought me those Mary Janes, which I wore with great pride, although I was allowed to wear them only a few minutes a day. I have since worn many pairs of beautiful shoes, but I will always remember this gift of love and understanding.

—**SUSAN ELKINS IRGENS, Yorktown, VA, mother, daughter of Lou Elkins, U.S. Marine, golf pro (1924–1999)**

THE DATE

It would be tough for her first boyfriend to live up to this.

When I was four, my father took me on my first official date. My mother, who was busy taking care of my baby brother, told me that Daddy had a special surprise for me. So on a warm summer evening, for no particular reason other than Daddy taking his girl out, I got all dressed up in my prettiest pink dress and shiny black patent-leather shoes.

First we went to Neilsen's ice cream parlor in Port Chester, New York, for a banana split. I can still hear the clinking of my metal spoon reaching to the bottom of the glass dish that contained the most delicious banana split in town. Then he took me for a long ride in his black-and-white '57 Chevy with red interior to see the cows on King Street. He parked the car on the side of the road so I could get a good look at the big brown-eyed cows. I was so excited and so proud to be his date, and he made me feel so special to be his "little girl." To this day I am still proud to be his little girl, even if I'm not so little anymore. My dad was the strongest and handsomest man I have ever known, and he will have that title in my heart forever.

> —JOAN CARRIERO, Port Chester, NY, school secretary, daughter of Carmin Giammarino, millwright (1926)

THE COMFORTER

It's easy to forget that what seems minor to an adult can be monumental to a child.

When I was a little girl and my father put me to bed, it would always be cold in the room—especially the sheets—and he would wrap my feet in my baby blanket to keep them warm. Before he kissed me, I had a litany of things I went through every night: "Can I call you if I need anything? Can I call you if I get hot? Can I call you if I get cold? Can I call you if I get scared? Can I call you if I get hungry?"

He would listen and say yes after each one, and I would fall asleep, secure that I was completely loved and cared for.

—Anne White Foster, Richardson, TX,
realtor, daughter of Johnnie E. White,
school superintendent (1907–2004)

THE LETTER

U gotta just-a love this-a letter from a fadder to his daughter.

Although he is in his eighties, my father, a first-generation American of Greek descent, is still running a business and working every day from 7 A.M. to 5 P.M. His family struggled when he was young, and although he was gifted both academically and athletically, he was unable to attend college. He sacrificed to help support his younger siblings—there were nine of them—even as his own young family was growing.

He was a man of few words who expected a lot. I was always pushing him for more freedom, and he was always trying to rein me in without breaking my spirit. I was the first in my family to go to college, and a month or so after I started my freshman year, he sent me a letter that is still dear to my heart.

He began with the comings and goings at

home and went on to tell a funny but poignant story about an immigrant father and his son. My father wrote:

Joe Spinelli gave his son Dominic a black onyx ring when he left for college. It was a very expensive ring. Dominic was thrilled, but when he looked at the inscription F.U.F. inside the band, he was somewhat puzzled.

So Dominic asked his father, "How come? My name is Dominic. What does F.U.F. stand for?"

In broken English, the old man replied, "From-a U Fadder."

I don't believe there's a moral, except that this letter is F.U.F., From-a U Fadder. I've got to tell you exactly how I feel about your being away from home, if I can only find the right words.

There's this father who never had children before until the first little girl came along. Picture her something like you. All through her growing up, her father tries to do for her all the things that he feels are right. Trying very desperately to help her overcome the problems she encounters in her childhood, and trying to instill in her all the good characteristics that he has and **none** of the bad. Giving her a little more freedom each day in almost immeasurable amounts and, with that little freedom, a little more responsibility to go along with it. Never swayed by what others close to the family brought up in the way of criticism for being too strict, too stingy, too easy, or too foolish.

Finally, after seventeen years, the father, with so much more to tell this now–young lady, fails to tell her anything. One day, he takes her away to school, and again, with so much to say, he says nothing. But all the time he's thinking, and it goes like this. . . .

"Here she is and I'm leaving her. Did I teach her well? Has she listened to me? Have I set a good example? Can I leave her? Will she be all right? Will she know what to do? Does she know why she's here? Does she want to be here?"

All my questions have really been answered. . . . All I want for you is that you fully develop all of your capabilities to the point that no matter what the future has in store for you in the way of happiness, sorrow, children, marriage, grief, and unhappiness that you will face it and have the resiliency to bounce back and face life as it really is and to pass on to your children what has been passed on to you. So there. I'm proud of you. See you in a couple of weeks.

From-a U Fadder

Even at seventeen, I knew my dad had given me a very special gift in the form of this letter. I went on to law school, marriage, and three children. My marriage fell apart, and my dad and his words of encouragement, set out in this forty-year-old letter, helped me through years of single parenthood, tuitions, and teenagers. He didn't often express his feelings, but he never failed to show up for a special occasion and many not-so-special occasions. He was always the first to sing "Happy Birthday" to my children each year, even if it meant rousing them out of bed in a college dorm.

When I received this letter, I had no idea that my future would entail so much heartache. My dad taught me to never give up. There was only one expression that was taboo in our house when I was growing up, and that was **I can't.** Today, my three daughters have all finished college. They, too, have known hard times, but they are survivors. My dad has challenged all of us to be strong in the face of adversity and to adapt to the inevitability of change. He remains and will always be my mentor, my guiding light, my dad, my fadder.

—ELIZABETH WEBER, Lynn, MA, attorney,
daughter of Milt Dadoly,
small-business owner (1923)

Honor

"He who stands for nothing will fall for anything."

—JOHN CARR,
father of
David Carr

President Harry Truman and General Douglas MacArthur were bitter rivals, to the point where Truman relieved MacArthur of his command during the Korean war. And yet both men—the common man who found himself in a position of great power, where he had to make uncommonly hard decisions, and the feisty and brilliant military leader—were heroes to my dad.

When I was twelve, General MacArthur gave a speech at West Point that became an instant classic, especially in our neighborhood. Dad referred to it often, and to this day whenever I hear the word **honor** I think of MacArthur. His subject that day was "Duty, Honor, Country"—the motto of the United States Military Academy. To some people, MacArthur told the cadets, those words were just a slogan. "But these are some of the things they do," MacArthur said. "They build your basic character. They mold you for your future roles as the custodians of the nation's defense.

They make you strong enough to know when you are weak, and brave enough to face yourself when you are afraid." It was a great speech, and I'm sorry it isn't better known today.

After **Big Russ & Me** was published, one of my readers sent me a quote from General MacArthur that he thought I might enjoy. "By profession I am a soldier and take pride in that fact," MacArthur said. "But I am prouder—infinitely prouder—to be a father. A soldier destroys in order to build; the father only builds, never destroys. The one has the potentiality of death; the other embodies creation and life. And while the hordes of death are mighty, the battalions of life are mightier still. It is my hope that my son, when I am gone, will remember me not from the battlefield but in the home, repeating with him our simple daily prayer, Our Father Who Art in Heaven."

I was both surprised and impressed that this great soldier had put an even greater value on fatherhood. But when you think about it, some of the qualities of a good father are not all that different from the attributes of a good soldier. Both jobs require hard work, sacrifice, patience, loyalty, and honor.

Some values are taught with words. As the

stories in this chapter make clear, others, like honor, are transmitted mostly by example.

In the spring of 2005, I interviewed three justices from the United States Supreme Court. Antonin Scalia's father had been a professor of Romance languages, and I asked the justice what he had learned from his dad. Although Eugene Scalia had been an intellectual who spent time with other intellectuals, Justice Scalia made it clear that his father had answered to a higher authority. "Brains are like muscles," the professor told his son. "You can hire them by the hour. The only thing not for sale is character."

MacArthur himself couldn't have put it better.

THE TICKETS

Doing the right thing—priceless.

My dad is the biggest New York Giants fan alive and has had season tickets for over forty years. In 1990, he took me to the NFC championship game against the 49ers. He had four tickets, and he planned to sell the other two.

We got to the game early to tailgate, and as we were pulling into the parking lot, I noticed that tickets were being scalped for hundreds of dollars. My father was going to make a killing, which was good because business had been difficult and he could really use the extra money.

We tailgated for a couple of hours, during which Dad must have had twenty-five different opportunities to cash in on his tickets, but he made no effort to sell them. I realized that he would probably get top dollar closer to kickoff, and I watched him carefully, hoping to learn a thing or two.

As the start of the game approached we headed for the stadium entrance, and my father continued to pass up selling opportunities. I remember thinking that maybe he was getting greedy. But he was looking around and finally saw what he wanted—a father and a young boy who needed tickets. My father explained that he had two extras and was just asking what he paid for them.

"Are you serious?" the man asked.

"Yes," my father replied. "Now let's go in before we're late for the game."

I did learn something that day—something about having principles and doing what is right. I know today that my father got more enjoyment out of seeing that father and son watch the game right next to us than if he had sold each ticket for a small fortune. In doing so, he taught me a lesson I will never forget.

—**BRIAN BAKER**, Raleigh, NC, **equities trader, son of Bob Baker, printing salesman (1939)**

THE LOAN

Every now and then, a father says something really important. And once in a great while, a son is listening—and learning.

I recall a moment of clarity that I experienced with my dad when I was twenty-one. I was going to college and living with a couple of buddies in Minneapolis.

When the car I was using died, my dad, realizing that I needed transportation to get to work and to school, was good enough to lend me the money for a used Chevy Citation. Shortly after I bought it, my parents drove down to San Diego for the winter. Before they left, my dad gave me a short stack of his bank deposit slips with explicit instructions to put one hundred dollars of my earnings, every payday, into their savings account while they were gone.

At that time of my life, my priorities weren't exactly straight. I dismissed our agreement as trivial and continued to spend my money as fast as I was making it, in pubs, on dates, and so on. Instead of honoring our agreement, I made payments that were less than the agreed-upon amounts, and on more than one occasion I made no payment at all.

When my parents arrived home in late March, I got a call from my dad, who said, "Don't go anywhere. I'm coming over." My dad was (and still is) a physical presence and had been a trucker for thirty-five years. I felt ashamed and guilty, knowing that Dad had discovered that I hadn't held up my end of our bargain.

After he came in, he told me to sit down because he had a few things to tell me. There was no yelling, no red face with a vein about to burst on his forehead, and no swearing. His first words were, "When your mother and I got back into town yesterday, I called the bank. I can't say I was surprised to discover that you hadn't made all the payments. My first thought was to come here and take the car from you, but I want to tell you some things while I'm here. Maybe you'll understand, and maybe you won't."

He went on to tell me, very calmly, about what it means to keep your word and honor your commitments. He explained that when he was growing up after the Depression, a man's handshake and his word meant everything. He also told me that because I was twenty-one, he didn't feel angry so much as sad and disappointed. He closed by saying that our words and actions have a real effect on others, and that my words and actions were a yardstick that others would measure me by. He added that if I hadn't yet formed some core values and principles, this might be a good time to start thinking about those things.

For the first time, I saw genuine disappointment on Dad's face.

He gave me a second chance to make our deal right, and even gave me more deposit slips, saying, "I will take those keys if you miss a single payment or, at the very least, if you don't let me know in advance that you'll have trouble making a payment. I understand that things can happen."

He spoke for about forty-five minutes, and I listened. He didn't expect me to say much, and I knew enough to keep quiet. I just nodded or shook my head at the right time and continued to listen.

That time we spent together changed me forever. Then and there, I made a commitment to myself that I'd never again be the cause of that look of sadness and disappointment on Dad's face. After that defining afternoon, our relationship got better and better.

I'm now married with two sons of my own, and they're already learning about the importance of honor, trust, and honesty.

—DAN BROWN, Taylors Falls, MN,
HR director, son of Donald O. Brown,
truck driver (1929)

THE PACT

He made a solemn vow, and without any fanfare he honored it.

Many years ago I was dating a girl in my hometown of Adamsville, Tennessee, whose father and mine had been classmates. One Saturday night when I went to pick up Becky, her father asked me how my dad was doing. I was only twenty-one, and I made some smart-aleck remark that I no longer remember. I had always been embarrassed about my father's humble job, because I knew he could do better, and Becky's father was the most successful man in our village. But he told me a story that night that gave me a whole new understanding of my father.

My father and his twin brother were born prematurely in that same town. They were born at home, as there were no hospitals in the early 1920s in that part of Tennessee. The doctor told their parents, "Just keep those boys warm and love them while you have them, which won't be long." (They had already lost two other sons at birth.) Three weeks later, when the twins were still alive, somebody decided to weigh them. They were all of three pounds each.

Fast-forward to 1944 and the Battle of the Bulge. Both brothers served under General Patton in the Third Army and were captured a few days before Christmas. In the POW camp, my Uncle Frank became very ill and was running a high fever. The Germans were starving their prisoners (my father would eventually drop from 135 pounds to 95 before the war was over).

My father feared that his brother would die in the prison camp, which was by no means uncommon. Becky's father told me that one night before bed he got down on his knees and asked God to spare him and his brother, saying that if they could go back to Adamsville alive, he would never ask for anything ever again and would accept whatever God gave him.

It was thirty years later that I heard this story, and suddenly everything clicked. My parents were deeply religious, and my father had more friends than anyone I knew. His word was good with everyone in town, and he was the happiest ex-POW I had ever seen or read about. He had accepted the first job he was offered in a garment factory, although it wasn't a glamorous position and it didn't pay well—just minimum wage plus overtime. (My mother worked at the same factory for over forty years.) My father had made a pact with God, and as far as he was concerned, God had kept His part of the bargain.

Becky's father went on to say, "When we were young, everyone thought your father would be a senator or a governor because of his personality. We thought he might be a great businessman, like your grandfather, but that was before we knew that he had made a promise to the Big Guy upstairs. I respect your father more than any man I've ever met, because he chose the high road, and he kept his word forever. Not many people can do that, son. You've got a dad that anyone would be proud of."

From that day on, I felt privileged just to know the man.

—TED B. DONALDSON, Memphis, TN, investment broker, son of Grady Donaldson, factory worker (1922)

THE GOOSE

A lesson is learned—a generation after it was taught.

One night, when I was a teenager, my friends and I stole a goose from a lady who lived near the woods where we played. The next day we took it down by the river, near Dad's farm, to cook it. While it was on the spit and the drift-wood fire was sizzling, it was determined that the goose would need some salt, so I was elected to cross the fields and go into Dad's barn for some of the rock salt he occasionally gave to the cows. Even the salt didn't help; we couldn't keep the fire hot enough for long enough for the goose to get totally cooked.

Despite our poor results, we ate some of the goose and headed back to town and school.

Several weeks passed, and one day word came to me that the lady who owned the goose wanted to see us. (She was the aunt of a cousin of mine, so I knew her.) She saw us one at a time. I don't know what she told the other boys, but my conversation with her was kind and gentle. "Rex," she said, "I'm very disappointed in you. Your mother is one of my dearest friends, and I know she would be saddened if I were to tell her that you stole my goose. You do not want to be known as a thief, so this will be our little secret, if you promise me you'll never steal anything again." Of course I promised.

After I was married and had teenagers myself, I would often visit the Goose Lady, and each time I thanked her for teaching me the lesson of a lifetime. On my last visit, shortly before she died, she told me how she knew I had been involved with the goose caper. She said that, long ago, my father had come to her and said he had seen me take salt from his barn. He followed me back to the river and witnessed the goose being cooked. She said, "Your father thought, and I agreed with him, that the message of 'Thou shalt not steal' would be more impressive if it came from the lady you stole from, rather than your parent."

My father had died in the interim, and I was sad that he had never told me of his role in the story. But now I can only be thankful for a father who, even when I didn't know it, was still watching out for me.

—**WILLIAM REX STEVENS, Eugene, OR,
heavy equipment distributor,
son of William Clayton Stevens,
dairy farmer (1888–1964)**

THE STADIUM

This father was able to convey a powerful life lesson with nothing more than the slight pressure of his hand.

As a twelve-year-old boy in 1942, I was excited about the promise of a professional baseball game on a hot summer night in Oil City, Pennsylvania. My father, a hard worker with a heavy six-day-a-week schedule, had rushed through the day so he could take me to the game.

As we approached the stadium, the wide doors near the right-field bleachers opened to accommodate the moving of a giant road scraper. Dozens of fans angled toward the opening, some commenting loudly about a free baseball game. Thinking this was our lucky night, I leaned toward the open doors, but my father's firm grip determined otherwise as we continued toward the ticket line.

The action on the field and the winner of the game are long forgotten, but not the silent message of honesty from a loving and disciplined father.

—FRANK E. CARLSON, Houston, TX, benefits manager, son of Elmer F. Carlson, bread salesman (1900–1943)

The Teacher

"Setbacks are just opportunities to rethink your position."

—DAVID OVERBAY,
father of
Andy Overbay

Some of my dad's teachings had to do with how you carried yourself, while other lessons were more practical: how to shake hands ("don't give the other person a wet fish"), how to shovel the driveway, and how to drive—especially in bad weather. To hammer home that driving in the rain required extra care and attention, he filled a shot glass with water and poured it onto the kitchen floor. "Just look how that little bit of water spreads across the floor," he said. "Now imagine what two inches of rain will do to a road."

For former secretary of state Madeleine Albright, an important teaching moment with her father occurred when she was seven years old. Josef Korbel was a diplomat and a professor whom his daughter describes as "extremely demanding and totally loving." In England during World War II, Madeleine's school sent out report cards with extensive comments. Her grades were fine, except for a D minus in geography. Professor Korbel noticed the grade and read the teacher's comment: **Madeleine is discouraged by initial difficulties.**

"I don't think the bad grade is as important as the comment," he told his daughter. "I never want anyone to say that about you again."

Sixty years later, Albright told me, she could still hear her father's voice. She added, "I am only sorry that he had not addressed second, third, or fiftieth difficulties."

When I interviewed Rush Limbaugh, I wasn't surprised to learn that his dad was quite a talker—to the point where some of Rush's high school friends used to come over to the house just to listen to him hold forth. The older Limbaugh, Rush told me, had one big regret: that his son dropped out of college after a year, which made him think he had failed as a father. As Rush tells the story, it wasn't until his father watched him on national TV, debating Al Gore on the environment, that he said to his wife after the show, "Where the hell did he learn that?"

"From you, silly," his wife replied.

It was only then, Rush said, that his father realized that he hadn't failed as a parent.

And when I asked Rudy Giuliani what he had learned from **his** father, I was amazed by his response: "My father used to tell me that in times of crisis, when people are getting very emotional, and they're very upset and they're crying, the most important thing is to be helpful to them, and calm, and to actually become calmer when things around you are getting more and more out of control."

Rudy Giuliani certainly heard his father's voice on the day it mattered most: September 11, 2001.

THE LESSON

The boy was only eleven, but his father wasn't afraid to talk to him about the big picture.

My father never missed an opportunity to impart one of life's lessons, even when we were just out walking, and sometimes especially when we were out walking.

One Sunday morning when I was eleven, we found ourselves ambling by Riverside Memorial Chapel on the Upper West Side of Manhattan. My father stopped right in front of the funeral home and asked me what time it was. I checked my watch and told him it was 10:25. Then he asked me what I saw going on there. Nothing very exciting, I said. Just a crowd of people, maybe 150 in all, going into the chapel.

My dad commended me for a good observation and we continued our previous conversation about the New York Giants. After a while, however, I realized that we hadn't moved at all. We were still standing in front of the funeral chapel.

Naturally, I asked why. My father didn't answer immediately, but soon he interrupted my talk of baseball with another question, as those who had entered the chapel earlier began to file out.

"What do you see now?"

I shrugged. "Well, I see all of those people who went into the chapel coming back out."

"Excellent," he said. "By the way, what time is it?"

I looked at my watch and reported that it was now 10:50.

My father nodded thoughtfully. "Well, that's about right. When a person's life is over, we have a funeral to celebrate that life, and it generally lasts about twenty minutes."

I was more than a little puzzled.

"Dad, I'm only eleven. Why are we even talking about this?"

"Because I hope you will live a long and productive life, that you will be aware of your surroundings, that you will stay out of trouble, and that you will be thoughtful and cautious. And above all, that you will always know in the back of your mind that someday your entire life will be summed up in twenty minutes."

—STUART FRANKEL, New York, NY, Wall Street trader, son of Adrian Frankel, securities trader (1910–1970)

THE BOX

If the letters I received are any indication, one of the subjects most often addressed by fatherly advice is a child's tendency to worry.

I used to be a chronic worrier. One day, when I was around thirty, married with children, my father came over with a little wooden box. He sat me down and said, "Wilma"—he always called me that—"when you have a worry, write it down on one of the pieces of paper in the box. Close the box and continue doing this for two weeks; write down all your worries and put them in the box." I did as he advised.

After two weeks, Dad came back, and together we opened the box and read the worries. All of them had either come to naught or were things over which I had no control. He taught me a powerful lesson, and from then on I worried much less. What will be will be. When he died, people told me he was the wisest person they had ever known. He didn't give advice; he provided solutions. I was so blessed to have him.

—TONYA STANFAR, Berea, OH, retired administrator, daughter of Frank Stanfar, salesman (1911–1991)

THE CODE

It's not just what Dad taught. It's how he presented it.

When I was very young, my dad introduced my brother and me to a special word: Essie. This was our own secret code, a subtle reminder to maintain our composure when something or someone might cause us to become upset, or an internal reminder if, because of peer pressure or bad judgment, we were considering veering from what we knew to be right. Over time we came to learn, as Dad told us it would, that Essie would help us cope with both difficult situations and difficult people.

A couple of examples come to mind. One was on the baseball field after the umpire made a call I thought was wrong. The other was a card Dad gave me when I graduated high school that said simply, **Remember Essie.**

It took my brother and me some time and experience to realize that Essie was Dad's way of packaging the idea of self-control, or S.C., for a couple of young and precocious boys who might have found that common phrase too dry or overly restrictive.

—TIM HANLON, Ridgefield, CT,
HR manager, son of Joseph D. Hanlon Jr.,
comptroller (1924)

THE ACCIDENT

Sometimes a father's lessons yield more than he ever imagines.

One of the most important lessons I learned from my father took place in our driveway when I was in elementary school. We used to play basketball every day, and he decided that I needed to learn how to shoot and dribble with my left hand. Being naturally athletic, I quickly became frustrated with my lack of left-handed success. Shot after shot clanked off the bottom of the rim or missed the rim entirely. I became very angry, lay down on the driveway, and began to cry, and my father stood there and looked at me as he waited patiently for me to get over my tears. When I realized that my behavior was not getting me anywhere, I got back up. He passed me the ball and I continued to clank left-handed shots off the bottom of the rim. His lesson of never giving up and working harder to accomplish my goals was conveyed to me without a word. I eventually became proficient with my left hand, but what I really learned that day was a road map for overcoming my biggest challenge in life.

When I was eighteen I was in a car wreck, where I cracked a vertebra in my spine and tore every major muscle in my neck. I was going to college to play soccer and be a decathlete on the track team, and now I was told that I would never walk without a limp and would never again be able to perform athletically.

For half a year I was not even able to put on my own underpants. (I had to use a hanger to pull them up.) I wanted to quit school and give up. I wanted to lie down and cry that life was unfair, much as I had done in our driveway so long ago. But every time I felt that way, that earlier memory danced in my mind. I knew that if I was patient and continued to work hard—**very** hard—I could overcome this obstacle.

For three years I continued to go to school, doing three to four hours of painful rehabilitation every day, with constant support from my parents. And I finally earned my way back on the playing field. This time it was football instead of soccer, because that was my dad's favorite sport; I chose football to honor him and give him some small thanks. I didn't tell my parents that I was trying out for the college team until I made it.

In the second game of the year, I kicked my first field goal—forty-nine yards, a school record—and we beat the number-one team in our division. I looked to the stands, tapped my heart, and pointed to Big Rich and my mother in the stands. That lesson in the driveway had allowed me to be on the field that day, and I owed it all to my dad. I succeeded because of who my father is, and who I am because of him.

—JEFFREY S. KERNS, Dakota City, NE, educator, son of Richard P. Kerns, district manager (1948)

THE DREAM

Even after his death, he was still helping her.

I have been diagnosed with manic depression and have not had an easy life. At one point I was in such agony that I prayed to God to either help me get better or let me die. That night, my long-deceased father, who was killed in a plane crash when I was twelve, came to me in a dream. As I remember it, my eyes were shut as I envisioned his face in my mind. I didn't "see" him, but his comforting presence made the whole room feel safe. Gently he whispered, "This is not your fault . . . but it **is** your responsibility." I felt remarkably content during and after this dream.

I had sometimes told myself the very same thing, and so had other people, but the idea that this depression was not my fault was now somehow more believable. I can't claim I immediately got better, but my father's presence and his words really helped. Step by baby step, I started participating in life again. I knew I really had no other choice.

—SANDRA REAVIS, Rockaway, NJ, advocate, daughter of Walt Reavis, airline pilot (1915–1966)

ADVICE

Not many boys want to take dance lessons, but a lot of men wish they had.

I joke with my children that my father gave me only two good pieces of advice:

First, never go into the bar business, even though it may look glamorous. It's not.

Second, take dance lessons when you're

young, because if you're a good dancer, you can walk into any party and have the best-looking girl in your arms within five minutes.

—NORMAN SCHREIBER,
Williamsville, NY, car dealer,
son of Louis Schreiber,
nursery owner (1898–1960)

THE REALIST

It's a wise child who can recognize a difficult truth.

When I was seven, Dad would take me to visit Mom in the hospital. She had just had her leg amputated and was in a terrible mental state. One night, as we were taking Mom for a walk in her wheelchair, we ventured into a surgical area where we saw some very sick people hooked up to all sorts of machines. I was astonished and said, "Dad, these people look **really** sick."

"Yeah," he replied quietly. "Just remember that there's always somebody worse off than you are." I knew instantly that he said this for

Mom's benefit, but I also knew in my heart that it was a lesson for a young boy as well.

—**Bruce Fairclough**, Newington, CT, photographer, son of Benjamin Fairclough, factory manager (1912–1976)

THE ROOM

Dad gave her a choice, and in the end she chose the painful truth.

My father lived through the Holocaust. He had survived Auschwitz, the same camp Elie Wiesel had been in, and they were the same age. When I was fourteen I was reading Wiesel's **Night** in school, but I had no idea that the Auschwitz he wrote about, where he had lived for a year, was the same place my father had been. But I did wonder why Wiesel hadn't been as lucky or as clever as my father and his companions.

My father's place was a kinder, gentler Auschwitz. As he described it, there was never a moment where people were dying in front of him. The worst had happened the first night, when they killed his parents and his siblings.

But from that moment on, as he described it, things were "not so bad." He and the other boys kept outsmarting their Nazi captors, often by stealing food right from under their noses. As a child, I used to picture my dad in the cast of a black-and-white television show called **Oscar and His Merry Men Meet the Nazis.**

His four children, his **kinderlach,** as he called us, knew there was more to the story. We knew our playful and brainy father had lost both parents, three younger sisters, and his older brother at Auschwitz. We knew which ones had died just a few hours after Dr. Mengele's "selection," and how Mengele, with his blue eyes, stared each inmate down as he decided who would live and who would die. We also knew who had survived—at least for a while—and who died just before the camp was liberated. But we didn't know their names. We didn't know what they looked like. We didn't know how the children sounded when they were torn from the arms of their parents. My father didn't want to frighten us. He wanted his children to feel safe in America, "the best place to live."

But when he was very, very sick in the hospital, and I knew we were losing him, I realized there was no going back. If I didn't make my move now, I could never again have access to his memories. If he died now, I would lose not only my father, I would also lose all the answers he held. Although he was very tired and sick, I said, "Dad, I need to ask you about your time there, in Auschwitz. I need to ask you some things. It's important."

He looked at me with real anger in his eyes. "Debbie, from the time you were a little girl, you always asked your questions. And I always told you, 'We got food, we got bread, we divided it up, we didn't suffer. It was fine.' And you kept bothering me and asking me these questions. And I kept telling you, as if I were in a room, 'Go away. Stop knocking on the door! I do not want to let you in this room.' And yet you keep coming back, saying, 'Let me in.' So I'll ask you one more time to go away. If you knock again, this time I'll let you in. But if I let you in this room, Debbie, you will never, ever, get out. So: Do you want to knock again and come in?"

I said, "Yes, I do, Dad." He was crying. He had covers on his body because he was very skinny and weak at that time, but he kicked off all the covers as if he were kicking down a door. "Fine," he said. "Come in, then. Come into a room that you can never leave."

"Can I ask you my questions?"

"You're in the room. You can ask me anything."

I asked him everything I ever wanted to ask. I asked him to tell me the real story, and he did. It was painful. And scary. And sickening. I felt that part of me had died.

My father was right: Once you're in that room, you can't get out. It's always with you.

—**Debra A. Fisher**, Rye Brook, NY,
occupational therapist,
daughter of Oscar W. Fisher, importer
(1928–1993)

THE TOWER

Years later, a father's boyhood experience continues to inspire his son.

When I find myself facing difficult circumstances, I think of a story I heard from my father about his boyhood in Nebraska.

"I remember the day I went up the water tower outside our town of Kearny. To a six-year-old boy, this tower stretched into the sky like Jack's bean stalk, with a ladder that begged to be climbed.

"My older brothers were not there to stop me, and before I knew it, I had gone up several rungs. It seemed easy, so I just kept going until I finally made a big mistake: I looked down! The ground was dizzyingly far below. I was completely frozen, incapable of moving. Panic set in. How would I get down? I'll be up here forever, I thought.

"But then I thought, Don't be ridiculous. Of course I won't be stuck on a water tower the rest of my life. Somehow, some way, by bedtime tonight I will be under the covers like always. I just don't know right now how that will happen. And, of course, I was right."

I sometimes find myself up the water tower in my own life. Budget cuts at my university left me unemployed at age fifty; a hand injury ended my career as a classical pianist; other problems rise up as regularly in my life as in anyone else's.

But I continue to draw comfort from the wisdom of that six-year-old boy in the Nebraska countryside, frozen with fear but knowing that everything would turn out all right. The thing that touches me most, however, is that my daughter feels the very same way about her grandfather's story.

Dad never did explain how he finally got down. The point is that he did.

—GLENN WINTERS JR.,
Newport News, VA, musician,
son of Glenn Winters Sr.,
lawyer (1909–1998)

The Character

"When I was in college, he sat down at my men's chorus concert and asked when the beer vendor was coming."

—Vince Guerrieri, son of Chuck Guerrieri

Reading through the letters that came in, I was pleasantly surprised by the number of sons and daughters who wrote candidly—and often lovingly—about unusual, eccentric, or deeply flawed fathers, men who might best be described as real characters. They include a man who played golf without ever buying a ball, a father who gave his daughter wildly inappropriate gifts that may not have been acquired in conventional or legal ways, an engineer who operated on the family cat (successfully), and a man who, when complimented on his two fine sons, liked to say, "They were raised by wolves." Another father told his new son-in-law on the day of his wedding, "You love Annie and never hurt her. If you ever do, I will kick your ass. Have a nice honeymoon."

And then there was my father-in-law, a man I never had the pleasure of knowing because he died before I met Maureen. Karl Orth had been a college football legend in his day. During the 1930s, he played for the St. Mary's

Galloping Gaels under their legendary coach Slip Madigan, who had played under Knute Rockne at Notre Dame. Karl was a big man: six feet four, two hundred and thirty pounds, which was **very** big for that era. He was also very religious and was known to risk a delay-of-game penalty because he sometimes insisted on praying in the huddle. He had many friends, most of whom he kept close, which may explain why his favorite expression was, "Save six for pallbearers."

Karl used to frequent Molloy's, a tavern in Colma, California, just south of San Francisco, which has been around since 1864. Molloy's is near the local cemetery, and Karl and his friends would end up there after a funeral. One day at Molloy's, a man in the bar began making disparaging comments about the Galloping Gaels. Karl asked him to stop, but the inebriated customer continued his attacks. Finally, the story goes, Karl made the sign of the cross, said a Hail Mary, blessed himself again, and proceeded to dispose of the heckler with a single punch, prompting a member of the beer hall congregation to mutter, "Well, I guess God willed it."

THE DIAGNOSIS

This is one of my favorites—especially the last line. There's a big laugh here, although (or maybe because) the subject is so serious.

Mother let me into the small apartment. When I asked her how Dad was doing she simply rolled her eyes, pointed to the living room, then darted into the kitchen.

Dad sat in his favorite chair. He was listening to Al Jolson singing "You Made Me Love You."

As I entered the room he raised his finger to his lips and pointed to the ancient phonograph. I was pleased by the old man's appearance. He still had all his hair—a great shock of thick white curls that framed his large, ruddy, handsome face. His light-blue eyes looked clear. Dad looked robust and full of good health, not like someone dying of cancer.

I sat on the couch across from him and lis-

tened to the song. Dad was enjoying it so
much that for the moment I forgot I had come
to New York on a somber mission.

The song ended. He turned off the phonograph and pumped my hand hello.

"Dad, how are you feeling?"

"Great, couldn't be better."

"I spoke to Dr. Grudin a couple of days ago.
He told me you have a problem."

"I **had** a problem. Its name was Grudin."

"Dad, be sensible. Your problem isn't
Grudin."

"I'm not going back to him. End of problem!"

"Your prostate needs to come out."

"It's not coming out. It's a great prostate!
Been with me for three quarters of a century.
That's reliability!"

"It's cancerous. You know that."

"Oh, cut the crap, Don. I'm seventy-five
years old. I feel great. I haven't an ounce of fat
on me."

"Dad, you're not making any sense."

"Grudin is an alarmist. I'll outlive him,
Don. Bet on it!"

"The operation is routine. Your prostate
has to come out. Why put yourself and Mom
through this?"

He sighed. "I appreciate your concern. I promise you this: The first time I can't pee I'll race back to Grudin and let him have my prostate."

"You know you won't tell a soul until it's too late. Surely this operation doesn't have you scared. Tell me the truth. Why aren't you having it?"

"Son, Grudin doesn't know my body like I do. He's wrong!"

"Dr. Roth told you it's prostate cancer. It took Mom two years to get you to Sloan-Kettering, and now the diagnosis is confirmed. Dr. Grudin says your prostate is the size of a grapefruit, and before long you won't be able to urinate. Your kidneys will stop functioning and that will lead to uremic poisoning. This thing can kill you, Dad! Your prostate needs to come out!"

He twisted uncomfortably in his chair. We looked at each other for a long time; then he breathed deeply.

"Son, it goes against my insides to talk about such things with you." The apartment was still except for the clinking sounds from the kitchen. "Did Grudin tell you the possible side effects of this operation?"

"No, what?"

"Impotence. The big 'I.' It's not only my prostate he's after. Even if it goes well and they get all the cancer, there's still a fifty-fifty chance of nerve damage, and that means no more sex."

The sound of clinking dishes stopped. Mother walked into the living room. She didn't look at either of us. "I have to run to the store for a few things. I'll be right back."

When the apartment door closed, Dad got out of his chair and walked over to me. "Don, if I can't make love to your mother anymore, I don't want to live. It's as simple as that. I'm not interested in peeing into infinity. I'm interested in making love to your mother till the day I die. And if I can't make love anymore, I'd **rather** die."

"Did you talk to Dr. Grudin about this?"

"No. He's an organic chemistry guy who probably never read Dylan Thomas or Gerard Manley Hopkins. He wouldn't understand what I'm talking about. He wants to keep me peeing while I want to keep on loving. Understand?"

"I understand. Remember, it was you who introduced me to Thomas and Hopkins. Though it's tough to admit, I do agree with you."

"God bless you, Don!"

He bounded out of his chair, flipped over the Jolson record, and turned the phonograph on.

I walked to the bathroom in the rear of the apartment to the sound of Jolson's rich full voice singing "Anniversary Waltz." As I closed the bathroom door, I heard Dad's voice join Jolson's.

"The world was in bloom, There were stars in the skies"

My father never had his prostate removed. He lived and loved another eighteen years after Dr. Grudin's diagnosis.

Dr. Grudin did not fare as well. He died of a massive stroke eight months after he diagnosed my father's cancer. Dad sent me a copy of his obituary from **The New York Times** with a note that read, **Grudin pees no more. Love, Dad.**

—**DONALD SCHEER**, Boynton Beach, FL, retired foreign service officer, son of Saul Scheer, printer (1905–1998)

THE BAD MAN

The first sentence of this letter was unique among all the submissions. Her father may have been a bad man, but he still taught her something.

My father was a bad man. He was a gambler, a pool hustler, an unfaithful husband, and a coal miner who believed that anyone who crossed a picket line deserved to pay the price.

I knew all this, but I loved that little man. He stood about five feet three inches, with jet-black hair, thick dark eyebrows, and deep brown eyes. I loved him even after he offered me a bribe to dump my fiancé so I could spend more time taking care of him after my mother died.

We lived in a small Pennsylvania coal town where not everybody loved my dad the way I did. One who didn't was the Very Rev. William J. Frawley, pastor extraordinaire of St. Valentine's R.C. Church. Father Frawley, a former marine chaplain, stood six feet tall. He had bushy eyebrows, piercing eyes, and a baritone voice, which he used to good effect in the confessional. You didn't want Father Frawley to hear your confession unless you didn't have anything to confess.

Dad and Father Frawley clashed often over the years. There was the Catholic Men's poker game, which my dad was winning quite handily when Father Frawley came over and asked Dad in front of the others why he wasn't donating more of his winnings to the church. Dad's response: "Well, what's a priest doing running a poker game?"

Then there was the time he and my mother got into a battle over Dad's purchase of a cemetery plot in a non-Catholic cemetery. She didn't think Father Frawley would approve, and she'd end up buried in unblessed ground, which meant she'd never get to heaven.

She called Father Frawley when Dad was three sheets to the wind and put Dad on the phone.

"Father Frawley? Fred Brown here. . . . Yeah, we're fine, Father. Father, I bought—yeah, I've been to mass, you just didn't see me; I'm easy to miss—I bought a cemetery plot over at Jefferson Cemetery. . . . Yeah, I know it's not a Catholic cemetery, but what my missus wants to know is, will you bless the ground? They didn't have any room in the Catholic cemetery. . . . I don't want to talk about it. Will you bless the ground? . . . I'm not coming over there. Just tell me, will you? . . . Oh, go to hell." And he slammed the phone down.

But even Father Frawley had to bend with the wind because land was running out. Mom died and was buried in blessed ground.

When my dad died five years later, I worried that Father Frawley wouldn't bury him. Dad knew he was dying and wanted "the exact same funeral your mother had." But we really weren't members of that church anymore. I'd been away at college, and Dad—well . . . the last recorded activity centering around our family was the day my mother was buried.

Father Frawley met with my brother and me in a small office that was just big enough for three hard-backed chairs and his desk. On top of the desk was an enormously large book. When opened, it took up the entire surface.

We went over the details of Dad's death. Then he took a ruler and ran down the columns of names.

"I don't see a Fred Brown listed here."

"Really? I can't imagine why."

"I see an Ann Brown."

"Yes, that's my mother."

"But this is five years old."

"Yes, it's been about five years since she died."

Then he turned to me and looked at me with those piercing, dark, unforgiving eyes that darted out from underneath his eyebrows.

"Did your father go to church every Sunday?"

I wasn't afraid. I met his gaze straight on. Priest or no priest, I was ready to lie.

"Yes, Father. Every Sunday."

"Then why isn't he listed as a contributor? There's not one contribution mentioned."

"Dad preferred to be anonymous and put the cash into the basket when it came around."

He stared at me a long time. There was dead silence in the room. I could hear my brother breathing, or maybe not. Maybe he'd stopped breathing just for those few moments.

But I never looked away. If my dad taught me one thing in this life, it was how to bluff.

Father Frawley slammed the book shut.

"Funeral will be Wednesday morning, nine A.M. And I expect to see a contribution envelope in the basket from you from now on, young lady."

"Yes, Father."

And so Dad had a great funeral and he lies next to my mother in peaceful sleep—I hope.

—SUSAN TISCHLER, Cape May, NJ,
reporter, retailer, daughter of
Fred W. Brown, coal miner (1905–1977)

LEAVE 'EM CRYING

It's not uncommon: You think you know somebody, and then you learn he had a completely other side.

They all think they know my dad. They say, "That sounds just like your dad." And they are right. They do know my dad.

They know him as the man at Kitty's birthday party. Needing someone to pop out of a cake like a Playboy bunny, they called Dad. They built a plywood and tissue-paper cake and gave him his costume—long underwear with a pink voile ruffle. Knowing he would lose his nerve, they also supplied a few drops of liquid courage. And so, three sheets to the wind, Dad didn't really pop out of that cake. He stumbled.

They know my dad as the man who hijacked a party. In the days of hijackings to Cuba, Dad's friend Donna hosted a "flyaway" party. Deciding that Donna's party needed a surprise, Dad and his sidekick, my mother, dressed in black with paint smeared across their faces. They snuck into the basement, flipped the switch that plunged the party into darkness, and kidnapped Donna. Leaving behind a briefcase wired with firecrackers and a ransom note demanding tequila with a worm, they calmed a hysterical Donna and made her party a hit.

They know my dad as the man who, just like Andy Hardy, said, "Let's put on a show" each Christmas for his department at work. One year he was Miss Piggy, another year he set the skit to rap music. He was the man who treated "his ladies" at work to lunch on his birthday. It started simply enough. When pantsuits first became acceptable for women, my dad said jokingly, "Couldn't you wear dresses in honor of my birthday tomorrow?" When every woman came dressed to the nines, Dad rewarded them with lunch. For the next twenty years, that lunch grew from a one-hour bite of food to an event. When his department grew to twenty-two women and was too large to drop in at a restaurant, he reserved party rooms around town. When the women suggested a little wine might be nice, the event moved to our house.

They know my dad as the man who coached all my brother's teams. In Little League, he had only two rules. Rule One: Parents had to keep their mouths shut. No yelling at the kids, the umps, or the coaches. Rule Two: Throw the ball home. Always. Tired of watching the ball go from third to an overthrown first base to an overshot second, his strategy was simple. Let them think they hit a home run. We'll get them out at the plate.

They all think they know my dad. But they are wrong. They don't know my dad. They don't know that as a young father with his own kids safely tucked into their beds, he received a phone call in the middle of the night from a distraught employee. Her daughter, a survivor of many suicide attempts, was missing. Would my dad help search? They didn't know that he sat in a car with the mother as the first light fell on Lake Olathe and the abandoned car sitting on the cliffs. They didn't see him as he waited while the lake was searched and the body recovered. They didn't see him come home hours later with bits of mud and morning dew on his cuffs. They didn't see him check on his own sleeping kids that gray morning.

They don't know that any scraped knee could be made better with his "There, there, there." Or that he cried so hard when he left me at college that he had to pull off the road. Or that he sat alone on the steps of our house as I left him after my wedding. They don't know that even after I was married, my dad would just happen to be in the neighborhood as he appeared at the hospitals to sit with my husband during my many surgeries.

They don't know that, at my brother's wedding, my dad followed the show-biz motto "Leave 'em crying." As he spoke about my brother, there wasn't a dry eye in the place. After my dad toasted my brother, saying, "I couldn't be more proud of you, and I love you dearly," my brother's tough-as-nails friends were red-eyed and jealous—jealous that he had a dad who told him, in public, what they had never been told even in private.

—RUSS ANN OPPERMANN, Olathe, KS,
girl Friday, daughter of
Lloyd Moore, aviation business
(1931)

THE GAMBLER

Not exactly a model father, but he was unforgettable—and, in his way, generous.

In a rooming house in Seattle, Charlie died alone. We hadn't been in touch for years when I learned this. Why had he moved from Oakland to Seattle? I asked his union steward. "Because he wanted to be near Longacres Racetrack. He wanted to be cremated and have his ashes strewn over the track, which was done." Perfect.

That was my father: an alcoholic and a gambler. I've made him instead a Damon Runyon character in my mind. My mother once told me she divorced him because "the bookies were threatening to kidnap you."

What I remember is standing beside him at Santa Anita yelling, "C'mon, my daddy's horse!" The one he bet on, not the one he owned. I was three, and he had kidnapped me and taken me across the country by train. My mother came to take me back, and he followed. In Chicago, we would walk to boxing matches amid a loud crowd of characters jumping from their seats to shout, spilling beer from paper cups, the women in fake furs and heavily made up. At six, with platinum-blond hair and my father's blue eyes, I must have seemed out of place, but I didn't know it. Walking home, Charlie would hold out his hand and rub his thumb against his fingers, saying, "Feel that air," while holding my hand with his other. As we walked, I sang, "Jesus loves me, this I know, for the Bible tells me so," as I'd been taught by my California grandmother.

Charlie didn't say much about himself. He did tell me, though, that the ship he served on during World War II had been torpedoed, and that only he and several others survived, rescued after two days and three nights in the dark—in the drink, he said.

Did he ever vote or drive a car? I don't know. But he did wake me one snowy night when he returned from working the night shift at the **Tribune**—it must have been midnight—to dress me warmly and take me for a ride on my sled.

He wore a suit and hat to his blue-collar job. From various venues he sent me age-inappropriate gifts, such as a Royal portable typewriter when I was seven and a strand of real cultured pearls when I was eight—which I later realized he had probably bought from a fence in a bar in Detroit. At the time, though, this seemed normal.

Sometimes he'd visit, and sometimes I'd visit with him at his brother's in Ohio. At seven, I went to live for good with my mother's parents in a Chicago suburb, where Grandpa Gilbert read to me whenever I wanted him to and let me play in the leaves he had raked.

Still, Charlie was my father. Yes, he left me for whatever his reasons. He left me his love of words and his good genes—my grandmother died at ninety-six and her sister at ninety-eight—and many memories: some heart wrenching, others heartwarming. He left me, too, his independence and somewhat antisocial attitude. I didn't know him nearly as well as I ought to have, but I do know that while I drink hardly at all and cannot bear to gamble, probably because my mother actually took my nickel when I lost a bet to her at the age of five, I am **so** my father's daughter. Still.

—JUDITH PETTIJOHN MCCONNELL,
Chicago, IL, student,
daughter of Charles Elbert Pettijohn,
newspaper mailer (1915–1983)

THE JOKER

He will always think of his dad with a smile—or more often, a good laugh. What a gift!

My father is deeply ridiculous. He's not above doing the wave when his son is in a spelling bee or is inducted into an honor society. When a nosy aunt inquired if I had a girlfriend, he told her I had several women to satisfy my physical urges but nothing serious. When I was in college, he sat down at my men's chorus concert and asked when the beer vendor was coming. In high school, he was the parent that my friends wanted to come with us on field trips.

Between my father and his father, a man who was known to yell across a crowded store or church when he lost sight of you, I have a very high threshold for embarrassment. I gave up being embarrassed about my father around the end of high school, but I didn't truly appreciate his silliness until his father died. "I can't cry for him," my father said. "I think of the things he did, and I start laughing!"

My father was an altar boy when they still said the mass in Latin. When he held the paten under his friends, he'd slap them on the chin. He'd loosen the bells after mass so the altar boy at the next mass would shake them during the consecration and lose them all over the place.

But beneath the irreverence and the silliness, he wears a Catholic workingman's sense of honor. Scratch a cynic, they say, and you get an idealist. It might not be in this lifetime, he told me, but the guys in the white hats always win.

I was a reader in church in college, and one passage, from the Gospel of Luke, resonated with me. Jesus said, "When you have done all you are ordered to do, say, 'I am a worthless servant who has done no more than his duty.' " My father wears a sense of nobility and an ability to do the right thing, not out of personal gain, fear, or guilt but because it is his duty.

Because he's doing nothing more than his duty, he doesn't accept praise well. When someone told him he had two fine sons, he said, "They were raised by wolves."

A friend of the family, who knows a little about bearing crosses, told my father at one point that he was due a special place in heaven.

His response? "All I was trying to do was get out of a little purgatory."

—VINCE GUERRIERI, Fremont, OH, journalist, son of Chuck Guerrieri, nurse, claims worker (1954)

THE GOLFER

He taught his son to be frugal in a most unusual way.

Although my dad wasn't the most talented golfer in the world, he was one of the most unusual. What separated Dad from other golfers was not his swing or the clubs he used. It was his ability to play the game without ever purchasing a single ball. He let other golfers buy them and lose them for him to—eventually—find.

I was about seven when he started taking me with him when he golfed. Before I learned how to properly grip and swing a club, Dad taught me how to spot balls and use the retriever to pull them out of ponds without falling in. I can still remember the joy I felt when I presented Dad with a flawless Titleist that I plucked skillfully out of a water hazard. He made me feel like I found a gold nugget instead of a little white dimpled ball worth about a dollar.

A few years later, Dad and my brother Mark taught me how to play golf as I walked alongside them during many pleasurable days on the course. I always was amazed how my father consistently found golf balls in the most obscure places imaginable—stuck between tree branches, in piles of leaves, under rocks, and in other places where regular people would never look. Once he spotted a brand-new ball tightly lodged under a tire of a car in a mall parking lot that was nowhere near a golf course.

He had an unusual way of keeping score. "How'd you do, Dad?" I'd ask him. "Eight over and one under," he'd reply. This meant he shot eight over par, and his inventory of golf balls had dropped by one unit.

He was meticulous about separating good, unscathed balls from uglier ones. Dad called the inferior ones "water balls," because he didn't mind losing them on holes with water hazards. He kept balls in egg cartons and plastic bags and always had plenty in his golf bag—until the day he had no balls at all.

One late-summer afternoon, Dad went out alone to play nine holes. When he got to the first tee and put his hand in the zipper compartment of his bag to pull out a ball, he came up completely empty. There were no balls in the trunk of the car either, but that didn't bother him. Instead of taking ten minutes to drive home to get balls or, God forbid, buying some at the clubhouse, my father came up with a more imaginative solution to his predicament. He stuck a tee (another item he never purchased) into the ground and hit an invisible ball. He continued with his virtual round of golf until he got to the third hole, where he found his first ball of the day. After nine holes, both components of his score were over par.

—ARTHUR FELDMAN, Ann Arbor, MI,
sales consultant, son of Jerome Feldman,
accountant (1921–1989)

THE INVENTOR

This dad gives new meaning to the old saying that there's more than one way to skin a cat.

He was an aircraft engineer, and in the evenings he could always be found tinkering in the garage. In front of our middle-class home he had ten Chevy Vegas, and he would switch parts on one to get another one running so he could sell it. Sometimes he'd take a carburetor he was working on and place it smack in the middle of our dining room table. While the family was eating dinner, he would try to figure out what was wrong so he could fix it. He didn't have to do this, but he was raised during the Depression and he knew the value of a dollar.

He was also an inventor. Because his kids all needed braces, he decided to make them himself. He boiled plastic football mouth guards and had us bite down long and hard to make a mold. Then he used a plastic cast to create the form. A combination of mold, leather strap, and rubber bands created a headgear that we only had to wear at bedtime, thank God. But it worked: We had straight teeth without orthodontia.

Dad thought he was going to be doing the world a favor, so he advertised in the local newspaper about making custom-made braces. Unfortunately, the authorities saw the ad and made an appointment. That's when Dad sat us down and told us he might be going to jail for practicing dentistry without a license. We were terrified, but he got off with a very stiff fine.

This wasn't the only time he decided he could be his own medical expert. When our cat developed a growth on the side of its head, Dad, with Mom assisting, decided to deal with it himself. He put the cat in a brown paper bag, and with the car running, added a little exhaust to knock the cat gently out. (I often wondered how he knew how much exhaust would be enough without killing the cat.) He opened the growth with a sterilized razor blade and drained it; then he sewed it up with a regular needle and thread. The cat was fine by that evening and lived five more years, until it was hit by a car.

—KARLA DISHON, Mission Viejo, CA, domestic engineer, daughter of Jack C. Craig, aircraft engineer (1925–2000)

Mr. Mom

"It's perfectly natural to honor the man who's been the only mother I've had for more than thirty years."

—Pat Frantz Cercone, daughter of Richard L. Frantz

When I started thinking about this chapter, I asked my sisters whether they remembered any families in our old neighborhood in which the mother left or died and the father brought up the kids alone. "Are you kidding?" B.A. said. "If somebody lost his wife, he just went out and got another one."

When I thought a little harder, I remembered that, for a few days in our house, Dad took over Mom's responsibilities. Our mother suffered several miscarriages, and at one point she was in the hospital for over a week, leaving Dad to care for us in addition to his two jobs. He left for work early in the morning, but first he set the table and had oatmeal and hot chocolate waiting for us on the stove—along with a note reminding us to clear and rinse the breakfast dishes. We used to come home for lunch and that week we went to a neighbor's, taking along our own lunches, which Dad had packed. By the third or fourth day, when he

had run out of peanut butter and bologna—
Dad had no time to shop—he made us tomato
sandwiches, which were a disappointment, to
say the least.

"Dad, just tomatoes?"

"No, tomatoes with lots of salt and pepper!"

He wasn't kidding, but if memory serves,
we all survived.

The first evening without Mom, Dad
brought home a prepared meal. But he couldn't
afford to do that more than once, so for the
rest of the week we all pitched in, making
meals and doing the various chores that defined Mom's day, and our neighbors and aunts
helped too. Even so, I can still remember Dad
cooking dinner, washing dishes, folding laundry, and vacuuming. Back then it was really
strange to see our dad in a domestic role.
Within a couple of days, however, Dad
seemed fairly comfortable at what was essen-
tially his third job. We helped him in every
way we could, and by the time Mom came
back, we had grown accustomed to our new
roles.

In those days, a dad who did housework
was something like a National League pitcher
today. You want him to be able to pitch, and if

he can hit a little, too, it's a kind of amusing bonus.

It's tough work to be a father and tough, too, to be a mother. When one man is doing both jobs—well, as these stories make clear, that's a monumental achievement.

THE CARD

It's hard enough for a single father to take on a mother's role. It's twice as hard when his only child is a girl.

Every year in May, my father finds in his mailbox a Mother's Day card from his only child. This may seem strange, but it's perfectly natural to honor the man who's been the only mother I've had for more than thirty years.

He's the one who taught me how to make homemade stuffing, successfully sew a zipper into a pair of pants, and combine just the right amount of flour and egg yolks to make noodles. That may not seem so unusual these days, when men are more sensitive and more flexible. But my dad took over mom duty when my mother died in 1974, well before the movie **Mr. Mom** made grocery-shopping, bread-baking, laundry-doing dads cool. And he took his mom role seriously.

When I was getting ready to graduate from

elementary school, my friends' mothers took them shopping for new dresses. My dad went to the fabric store and bought a pattern, shimmering material, and sewing doodads, then spent several hours huddled over the sewing machine to make a beautiful dress for me. When I was having trouble in sewing class making a pair of shorts, he not only helped me finish them but also made me a week's worth of shorts in bicentennial material so I looked really hip during the summer of 1976.

When I needed to take a treat to my school's bake sale, Dad headed to the kitchen, grabbed a tin of Hershey's cocoa, and baked a pan of brownies. His ego was boosted when those brownies were the first to sell out.

None of this was a threat to his manhood, even though men at that time were often judged by how cool they looked in their leisure suits or how well they danced the Hustle. His self-esteem was strengthened when, at sleepovers, I would model the flannel pajamas he made for me. He enjoyed the flabbergasted looks when he gave people gifts of homemade preserves.

Dad did all this while he worked full time, ran a household, and raised a daughter alone.

So each year, as I struggle to find the perfect Mother's Day card for him, it would be easier to forget it. After all, Father's Day is just a month later, right? **Au contraire.** One year I neglected to send a Mother's Day card, and I still hear about it. My father often says he's more proud of what he accomplished as my mother than as my father because being a mother was so much harder.

But if you think that means I can forget him on Father's Day. . . .

—**PAT FRANTZ CERCONE, Bradford, PA, communications director, daughter of Richard L. Frantz, barber, machinist (1938)**

THE COOK

Dad recovered quickly enough from heart failure. Learning how to cook took a little longer.

My mother died in 1972, quite suddenly, of a massive heart attack. She and Dad had been married for almost forty years, and he was devastated. The night of her funeral, my father was admitted to the hospital with heart failure and was in intensive care for a number of days. Things looked pretty grim—and then suddenly he recovered. When asked how he pulled through, he said he remembered that he had two girls at home who still needed him.

He became our cook while I went to work and my younger sister attended nursing school. Becoming our cook was no easy task, because he was unfamiliar with the kitchen and what went on there. Some days we arrived home to find the front door opened wide, which meant that dinner had burned and we would be eating in a restaurant. One day he called me at work at around 2 P.M. and said, "Doris, at what temperature, and for how long, do you cook chicken?"

I didn't know the answer—Mom had spoiled us all—so I told him to hold on while I checked with a co-worker. I got back on the line and said, "Three hundred and fifty degrees, Dad, for about an hour." There was silence on the other end of the line.

I waited a few seconds and said, "Dad, are you still there? Is everything okay?"

"Everything is fine," he replied, "but can you come home now? Your dinner is ready!"

—Doris Schluter, Locust Grove, VA, retired manager, daughter of John (Jack) Peter Schluter, chauffeur (1910–1973)

THE ASTRONOMER

If you ask me, the word of the day is un-conditional.

When my parents divorced in the late 1960s, I was three and my sister was one. At twenty-seven, willingly and lovingly, my father began raising his two little girls. His entertaining teaching methods actually made me look forward to our study time together—especially when we were learning about the solar system and one planet in particular. (You know the one.) He would point his finger first at me and then at his backside.

At one point he decided that my sister and I would learn one new word per day. I loved the day we opened the dictionary to **dolicho-**

cephalic. We still laugh about that one, but I actually remember what it means.

And I will always remember representing my elementary school in a state spelling bee. Dad and I spent countless hours studying the word list. I really thought I could go all the way, but I was eliminated early on. When I returned home after my devastating loss, under my pillow was a beautifully wrapped box. In the box was a gold bracelet and a note that said, **With ABSOLUTE love, Dad.** (Oh, so that's how **absolute** is spelled!) The bracelet is long gone, but twenty-seven years later, the note is one of my prized possessions. I still wonder how Dad got the gift and the note under my pillow before I raced to bed to wallow in my sorrow. He took my loss over **absolute** and replaced it with absolute love.

—PAMELA LAZARUS DAPPER,
mother, Tequesta, FL,
daughter of Howard Lazarus,
real estate (1942)

THE BAKER

Like a number of fathers in this book, he played the cards that were dealt him—and he played them well.

My dad was born in New Jersey in 1895, the baby of ten children born to German immigrants. During World War I, he served in France and Germany. We were poor, but life was good until the mid-1940s, when we noticed that his walking was unstable. He had developed a nervous disorder that we suspected was caused by exposure to mustard gas during the war; people said if they didn't know better, they'd think he was drunk.

He was a carpenter by trade, but now he was unable to work. The roles were reversed in our family, and he became Mr. Mom long before it became fashionable—a hard adjustment for an active outdoorsman. Mom went to work at a baking company, packing donuts on an assembly line.

Confined to home, Dad taught himself to cook and bake—he made awesome fudge—and how to sew, hook rugs, and so on. He did it all with a positive attitude, and he usually had a smile. When I started working, I would call him during the day. If he didn't sound cheerful, I would say, "Better get off the phone. I can smell your pie burning." Sure enough, when Mom and I got home we were greeted by a big smile, a twinkle in his eye, and homemade pie for dessert.

He found ways to overcome his disabilities. When my parents got a little dachshund puppy called Tiger, Dad figured out how to get him out during the day when Mom was at work: He taught him to climb in a basket, which Dad attached to the clothesline. Dad lowered the basket out the kitchen window, and when Tiger was ready to come inside, he hopped back in the basket and Dad pulled him in.

Dad continued to be upbeat throughout his life as he struggled from cane to walker to wheelchair before becoming bedridden. Through all his suffering, he loved life, family, and friends and was always ready for a party. He taught me to accept what life gives us.

—MAUREEN HARNETT, Tarpon Springs, FL, retired treasurer, daughter of Edward Schurr, homemaker (1895–1980)

THE TRANSFORMATION

He rolled two roles into one.

My parents had been together since the seventh grade. Their life on Cape Cod was wonderful and full, and they were grateful for their seven children, twelve grandchildren, and four great-grandchildren. They were very devoted to each other.

Early in 2004, Dad was hit with the blow of his life. His love, his soulmate, the woman he had taught to drive, cook, and swim, who had been his closest companion for more than fifty-four years, died of cancer at seventy-five. He and the rest of our family were devastated. Mom had always been the epitome of good health. Dad had battled prostate cancer and still smoked. Without Mom, what would he do?

The first decision he made was to remain in their home; he wanted her presence around him. Second, he got himself a dog. What happened next astonished us all. Dad changed. Always the rock behind Mom, he now began to take an active interest in the lives of his children and grandchildren. One of the first

things he did was to make a note of all birthdays and important family events—a simple
task, but never his. Then he started corre-
sponding with people. Write a letter or send a
card? Unheard of before this. He even started
cooking and cleaning, household tasks he had
never had to think about before.

He amazed us by adopting all the rituals
Mom had performed, and as time wore on he
sort of **became** Mom—giving advice for newborn grandchildren who couldn't get to sleep;
making daily phone calls consoling, advising,
and arranging trips to visit his children who
were far from home. Where did this inner
strength come from? Were Mom and Dad
having secret conversations in the middle of
the night? Is Mom still there, giving him inspiration and the will to go on? The connec-
tion between them was deep; we know that.
Their life together was a bit of a fairy tale. Was
it their era? Was it their upbringing in a time
where family and country were top priorities?
I think their greatest gift to their children was
their love and devotion for each other and
their pride in their country.

I salute my dad for continuing our family
traditions and going on with life as if Mom

were standing beside him. In some way, I guess she is.

—SUSAN C. LAJOIE, Orleans, MA, mother, daughter of Francis E. Lajoie, retired engineer (1928)

Hands (and Feet)

"I look at my father's rough, worn, and cracked hands, and I am reminded of the life he has lived."

—Krista L. Paternostro, daughter of Thomas A. Paternostro

Most of the chapter headings in this book seemed obvious to me even before I started reading the letters. But a few of them took me by surprise, and this one was completely unexpected. The idea for this section jumped out at me when I read Andy Overbay's letter, which included a reference to his father's "meaty paws." It was then I realized that, strangely enough, very few people wrote about their father's face, or even his eyes. But a number of writers focused on their fathers' hands.

I immediately thought back to the summer of 1998, when I was invited to address the annual convention of the New York State chapter of the American Legion. The event was held in Buffalo, and I was being given a journalism award. I began to talk about my dad, and referred to him as "the **real** Tim Russert." Big Russ and Luke were sitting together in the front row, and I noticed that Dad was wiping away a few tears with the back of his hand—

using that big paw of his to dry his eyes. And it wasn't just him, either. Many of the men in the room were wiping away tears with their hands—no handkerchiefs for these guys.

When I was a boy, Dad's hands did so much. He used them at work, of course, to lift trash cans and drive his truck, but at home they had a different purpose. Whenever my sisters and I acted up, Mom would swat us on the rump. "Keep this up," she would say, "and you'll have to deal with the Big Hand"—one of several nicknames for our dad, whose hands and forearms were very well developed from all his years of manual labor.

It wasn't just my dad who was defined by his hands; it was so many dads like him. One of the most poignant moments of my life in government occurred when I was working for Senator Moynihan and we attended a hearing in Buffalo about the plight of unemployed steelworkers. A big, burly man of forty-eight was testifying, and he was in tears. "Senator," he said, "look at these hands. These hands can still work! Give me some work, Senator. Give me my dignity." Everybody in the room was fixated on those big, empty hands, wishing there was some way to fill them.

I grew up at a time when just about every father, or so it seemed, was good with his hands and could fix basic plumbing or electrical problems around the house. Before you'd call a carpenter or a plumber, you'd fix it yourself, and if you couldn't, you'd bring in a neighbor or a relative. Every father in our neighborhood had a workbench in the basement and knew how to use it. But I guess not every trait is passed down through the generations. I have no talent in this area, which is a source of some amusement and occasional disappointment in our house—and considerable expense as well.

When I left Buffalo, moved to Washington, and started meeting people in government and in the media, something about them seemed different. And then it hit me: Their handshakes weren't as firm and their hands were much softer than the hands of the men I had known growing up. People speak of "white collar" and "blue collar," as if the difference lies in the shirt a person wears. Maybe so, but it also lies in their hands.

Just as I used to focus on my father's hands, Luke used to focus on mine. When he was little, at least once a year he would measure his hand against mine, palm to palm. I can still remember the smile on his face—and mine too—when his hand grew to become the same size as mine and then, a few months later, when it was finally bigger. It was another rung on a young man's climb to adulthood.

HERMIE'S HANDS

He proved that eight fingers were as good as ten.

Wisconsin winters can be harsh, but the people who live there are a hardy lot. My dad, known as Hermie, traveled the streets and side roads of Columbus, and at one point he delivered mail, a smile, and a joke to every citizen in the city limits and surrounding rural area. Even in winter, he rarely if ever missed a day of work. Handling large bundles of mail had to be awkward in such conditions, but he mastered it with only eight fingers.

When Hermie was twelve, an unfortunate accident removed the ring and pinky fingers of his left hand. But he refused to consider this a handicap.

Hermie used his hands to win the heart of my mom. In high school, he would stick the stubs in his nose and roll his eyes during class.

Later, Mom would often say, "I had to marry a guy like that!"

Hermie used his hands to drive a tank during World War II, where he was in the thick of many battles, including the Battle of the Bulge. He downplayed what he did in the war and the ten medals he received, but he never downplayed America. He considered it a duty and a privilege to serve.

After the war, Hermie used his hands to teach me a passion for sports—how to be ready for the pitch in baseball, how to get up after you've been knocked down in football, and how to hustle and never quit in basketball.

Around the house, Hermie used his hands to fix things. He also used them to make beautiful wooden items—tables, chairs, plates, and the family Ping-Pong table, which somehow folded up into a small storage space. Mom would often say, "Your dad never said he loved me, but he would always make me something, so I knew he did."

Dad's hands also demonstrated his love. They could touch your shoulder and make you feel better when you needed forgiveness. They could gather up the pieces when your heart was broken. And they could hold a family together when selfishness threatened to tear it apart.

Although we didn't always realize it, and although he had only eight fingers, Hermie's hands held our world together.

—JON HERMANSON, Knoxville, TN, department manager, son of Lawrence "Hermie" Hermanson, postal worker (1920–2004)

THE GLOVES

When you don't have much, you hold on to whatever you've got.

My large hands held my daughter just moments after she was born. That was the last time I was ever afraid I might hold her too tight. I touched Amy's puffy, pink face and said, "It's okay, little face, I've got you now." I touched her cheek and felt her warmth and a tiny pulse. I put her cheek to mine, sniffed her new smell, and cried for joy and relief.

My dad had probably held my sisters and me the same way. I don't know for sure, because he died when I was eighteen months new to the world, and to the life that he and my mother created for us. He was sick most of his life, but was strong enough to be a talented musician, a skilled surgeon, and a loving husband and father in the days before drugs and kidney dialysis became the lifesavers they are today.

He died just after Christmas in his thirty-sixth year. My mother believes he always knew his time was limited and that he tried to bring joy and life to us before it ran out. She says their twelve years together were a beautiful but too-short story. She says my hands are just like his, and that I look like him and make her laugh like he did.

I like the idea that my dad once held me in the same way I held Amy that day. As a young boy, I sometimes thought I heard his voice or his footsteps in the hall. I just wanted to see him. I know I am connected to him, and I can often feel his presence.

Not long ago, I came across his driving gloves in a small box of keepsakes. I slipped my hands into them and sat quietly at my desk, knowing this would be as close as I could get to his physical existence. The gloves fit me perfectly, as if I had chosen them myself. Maybe he wore them while driving us all to church. Maybe he matched them up with the tweed jackets and handsome wool suits I have seen in the few remaining pictures of him. The only smell is of aging leather, without what his signature scent might have been.

—JOHN BRINK, Duxbury, MA,
divinity student, son of John C. Brink,
physician (1912–1948)

THE CLOCK

His hands were clean, and so was his conscience.

Sometimes I would pick up Dad from work at Universal Studios, where he was a tool and die maker. He got off work at 3:30 P.M. When I arrived at 3:20, I noticed that all the men he worked with were washing up and heading to the time clock to punch out at 3:30. But my dad clocked out at 3:30 and then washed his hands. When I asked him why, he said, "They don't pay me to wash my hands."

He also liked to say, "I only work half a day—twelve hours."

—**PHIL ROBBINS**, Coeur d'Alene, ID, sales, son of Leo Robbins, tool and die maker (1923–1993)

THE KNUCKLES

These were the hands of a working man.

I remember my father's strong hands with slightly oversized knuckles, a common trait for someone who worked with tools. His hands were unusually clean, a rarity among automobile mechanics. Always, before leaving his shop, he followed a lengthy ritual of washing his hands, first with kerosene and then water, using a stiff brush and lots of Lava soap. He finished by carefully cleaning his fingernails with a pocketknife. The Lava soap, combined with the lingering smell of cigarettes, produced his unique odor—neither pleasant nor unpleasant.

As he aged, the big knuckles became even more pronounced and the victims of arthritis. The skin became more mottled with liver spots, and eventually those strong hands had a bit of a tremor, but to me, at least, they never lost their feeling of strength.

—DON SPRADLING, El Paso, TX, investment services, son of Al Spradling, car mechanic (1903–1991)

SIZE 17

He let his hands do the talking.

My dad was best known for his hands. Strong and hardened by years of exposure to every harsh environment imaginable, a handshake from Dad was still an adventure when he was seventy-nine. Twenty years as a tractor mechanic for the local International Harvester dealership, combined with decades of dairy farming, left him with meaty paws that snared your hand in his grasp. I was in grade school before I knew there was a way to clean your hands and face with something other than Lava heavy-duty soap.

I saw those hands bashed, mashed, and bleeding far too many times. I even saw the bone on one finger after an unfortunate encounter with a truck fan cowling. He lost his size 17 wedding ring to an injury that left his finger so swollen that the ring had to be sawed off. On the eve of our college graduation, my friends described meeting Dad as like shaking hands with a bear, and one of them insisted on showing me how Dad's hand had "swallowed" his own.

His hands were even the subject of discussion on a radio show, where a war of words had developed about the pros and cons of our government's support of agriculture. In response to a call from a woman who denounced farmers as "lazy welfare recipients," somebody called in a rebuttal. He didn't mention Dad by name, but his description left no doubt. He said that when you shook hands with Dad, "his hands are so rough that you hurt for what he must have been through, but at the same time you're proud to know that people like this still exist in America."

I can close my eyes and remember sitting at the breakfast table, listening to that broadcast with Mom and Dad. When the segment was over, Dad sat quietly in the corner; he looked at his hands and rubbed them. I don't know if he was proud or embarrassed, or a little of both. His eyes were clouded by emotion, but in typical Dad style, he said nothing. Then he went out and continued to do the things that had shaped those hands.

—**ANDY OVERBAY**, Chilhowie, VA,
extension agent, son of David Overbay,
farmer (1925–2005)

THE CRUTCHES

It's inspiring to read about fathers who were able to make light of their own disabilities, to the point where their kids grew up thinking that everybody lived this way.

My father, born in 1925, contracted polio at the age of five—the most severe kind, infantile paralysis. He was told he would never walk again, but he taught himself to walk with heavy metal braces and crutches. When I was four and met a friend's father for the first time, I asked her, "Where are your father's crutches?"

My brother once asked at the dinner table how old he had to be before he would get his crutches.

Sometimes we went to the beach. My father

could swim like a fish, but having no use of his legs he was easy to dunk under the water. It was fun for the moment, but payback was always tough. Getting him out of the water always ended in disaster. Two of us would carry him out and put him on a blanket so he wouldn't get all sandy pulling himself out and dragging on his bottom back to the blanket. He would invariably start to giggle, causing us to giggle, and eventually we would drop him in the sand.

We never saw him as having a disability. We would be holding a door for him and, like any other kid, we would say, "Hurry up, Dad!" People would look at us like we were horrible, but Dad would just laugh and say, "I'm coming!"

—DEBORAH CAMPBELL,
South Berwick, ME,
administrative assistant,
daughter of Robert C. Huse,
radio broadcaster (1925)

GENTLE HANDS

A whole life is conveyed in just three sentences—and two hands.

I look at my father's rough, worn, and cracked hands, and I am reminded of the life he has lived. He worked hard, sacrificed for his family, and struggled for everything he has ever had. But underneath that rough exterior are gentle hands that picked us up when we cried, carried us through the rough spots, pulled us up when we fell down, patted us on the back when we achieved success, and hugged us each night before we went to bed as he told us how much he loved us.

—KRISTA L. PATERNOSTRO,
Simpsonville, SC, association executive,
daughter of Thomas A. Paternostro,
child advocate (1939)

Being There

"It's never too late to begin the process of becoming the father you want to be, the one you always wished you had."

—ALLAN SHEDLIN JR.,
son of Allan Shedlin

In an often-quoted line, Woody Allen once said that 80 percent of success is just showing up. With apologies to Woody, I would amend that statement to read that 99 percent of parenting consists of just being there. Not long ago, I was at a sports banquet, where I sat with the great NFL quarterback Peyton Manning and his dad, Archie, another great quarterback, who was being honored that night. When it was his turn to speak, Peyton Manning stood up and said, "My dad always had a knack for making his children feel certain and secure." To me, that was another way of saying that Archie Manning was always there for his kids. And he must have done something right, because his two sons—Peyton and Eli—are both playing in the NFL.

Sometimes dads can't be around when they most want to be there. Because Big Russ worked two full-time jobs, he could never come to my Little League games. He would return from his first job around five-thirty and have supper and a brief nap before leaving for his second job, which started at eight. One afternoon, he came home and noticed I wasn't around. "Where's Timmy?" he asked Mom.

"He had a Little League game," she said. "I guess it's running late."

Actually, the game had started late because of a rain delay. I still remember that day. I finished my paper route and rode off on my bike to Cazenovia Park, the recreational center of our neighborhood, where I played second base for the Braves. I was halfway there when I realized I had forgotten to bring my belt, but I didn't have time to go back.

We were the home team, and in the bottom of the sixth and final inning, the score was tied. I was on second base when the batter hit the ball into right field. As I was rounding third, the coach yelled at me to keep going. Then, as I was streaking to the plate, my pants started falling down, and as I slid into home they were down around my ankles. "Safe!" yelled the umpire. My teammates were cheering as I slowly got up, elated and embarrassed at the same time. As I rubbed my poor, aching backside, I looked up. There, to my astonishment, was Dad, happily puffing on a White Owl cigar.

"Dad," I said, "it hurts so much."

And Dad, who wasn't really known as a poet, called back, "Never mind your bun. You scored a run!"

I thought of that day during the summer of 2005, when **The New York Times** ran a story about the Little League World Series. The game ended with a dramatic home run by Michael Memea of the West O'ahu, Hawaii, team, defeating Curaçao, 7–6. I was happy for the American kids, of course, but I was especially interested in one of their fathers. As soon as his son's team qualified for the World Series, Myron Enos, a truck driver, had asked his boss for time off to go to Williamsport. When his boss refused to grant it, Enos quit. "It was definitely worth it," he said. "It was a big sacrifice. But, you know, it was my family or my job. You only have one family. You can get plenty of jobs."

Over the years, I've spoken to a number of men who made a different choice, who put their careers first, and later wished they had been around more when their children were young. I'll never forget a conversation I had with former senator George McGovern, the 1972 Democratic presidential candidate. He had written a book called **Terry** about his daughter, an intelligent, compassionate, and funny woman who died of alcoholism at the age of forty-five. I read a lot of books, but this one was so sad that I had to put it down several times. As a father, it just tore me up, especially when McGovern quoted some of Terry's diary entries. In one of them, she addressed her father, saying, "Dad, I wish you were home more. Dad, I wish you could understand what I'm going through."

Although he was proud of his public service, McGovern was speaking for many sadder but wiser fathers when he said to me, "What I regret is that I didn't carve out more of those precious times to be with my kids. I really can't tell you how I regret that."

This chapter is about a group of men who didn't make that mistake, about fathers who, in one way or another, really **were** there for their kids.

THE SEMINARIAN

It's one thing to be there for your son. It's another to stand by him even when he breaks your heart.

My father, born in Ireland at the turn of the century, was so proud when my brother walked across the stage of All Hallows High School to receive his diploma, the first member of our family ever to do so. When I graduated three years later and told him I was thinking of going to college, he didn't know what to make of it. But when I told my parents a few weeks later that the college I was thinking of was the New York Seminary, I knew they were bursting with pride. In those days, nothing was more prestigious for an Irish family than for their son to head toward the priesthood.

My eight years in the seminary were long and difficult. As I entered my final year, there were a lot of necessary preparations for the ordination in May: the choice of a catering hall, the invitation list, the seating arrangements—it was just like a wedding but without the bride. The months went by quickly as my home parish, St. Anselm's, was gearing up for the Carroll family's big day.

As Christmas came and went, a faint but disturbing thought began to invade my consciousness. Did I really want to become a priest? Did I really want to take vows that would determine the course of the rest of my life? That year I had the privilege of singing a solo at St. Patrick's Cathedral during the Holy Week services. When it was over, I was allowed home for the remainder of the day. But my mom and dad had no time to speak with me. They were too busy finalizing the arrangements for my ordination, which was now only six weeks away.

Back at the seminary, my thoughts continued to haunt me, until I finally made the decision to abandon my goal and begin a different life. I had a friend who was already a priest and was stationed at a church about a mile from my home. I told him what I had decided, and he said he would leave a car on the seminary grounds so that after I made my decision known to the seminary authorities, it would be easy for me to leave. On a quiet Monday morning in April 1961, as the rest of the students attended classes, I slowly drove through the seminary gates into the streets of Yonkers, leaving an entire lifetime behind.

I went straight to my friend's rectory in the southeast Bronx. "What'll I do, Joe? How do I go home and tell them? It'll break their hearts." He volunteered to go to my house and speak with my parents first. He returned less than an hour later. "Tom, it's okay. It's time to go home."

I walked into that little apartment that I had known all my life. My parents were seated together on the couch. I just stood there; I had nothing to say. I started to cry, and to tell them I was sorry, and that I didn't know why I had waited so long. "Ye've nothin' to be sorry about, son," my father said. "Ye've done nothin' wrong."

As he spoke, the boxes of unmailed invitations were sitting off to the side as a cruel reminder of my unfinished obligation.

He stood up and faced me. "No one can live yer life for ye 'cept yerself. Musta been hard on ye these past months. Ye said nary a word to a soul. Me 'n' yer mother are prouda ye. 'Twas a tough thing ye had to do." I stood there, awkward and embarrassed. With a nod of his head toward the kitchen, he said, "C'mon, now. The tea'll be gettin' cold. You can be bringin' a cup to yer mam."

My mother died of cancer just three months later. My father lived for another ten years, but he never once brought up the topic again, let alone questioned my decision. He showed me right to the end of his life what it means to be a father. And I'll never forget that he was really there for me on the day when it counted the most.

—Tom Carroll, Mamaroneck, NY, retired college dean, son of Barney Carroll, stationary engineer (1899–1971)

THE HEISMAN

You wouldn't want to see a father do this too often, but once in a lifetime? What a memory!

My dad was born and raised in Ohio, and after World War II he attended Ohio State University.

I was in the eighth grade, sitting in math class, when I heard the school secretary say over the intercom that I should come immediately to the office because my father was waiting for me there. Of course I feared the worst, but when I saw him standing there, he had a big grin on his face. When I asked why he had come, he said, "Archie Griffin won the Heisman Trophy about an hour ago, and I wanted to tell you first." Archie Griffin was the great Ohio State halfback, and my father was so excited he just couldn't help himself.

—JEREMY KAHN, Olney, MD, sales,
son of Jerry H. Kahn, insurance broker
(1923–1990)

THE LATECOMER

There should be a first time for every-thing. Even at eighty-seven.

My dad took an earlier flight than he had planned, so he could get to the dock in time to see me shove off for my certifying exam in sculling. At eighty-seven, he looked incredibly robust, and he was carrying his camera to record this mini-milestone in a sport I had taken up only a week earlier, to commemorate my sixtieth birthday. I had always wanted to learn to row but had never had the time. I had always wanted my father to show an interest in my athletic endeavors, but **he** never seemed to have the time.

For decades I told myself that expectations for men in the 1940s and 1950s were different from today, and that fathers had not been expected to be much more than breadwinners and disciplinarians. But all my rationalizing did little to lessen the sadness I felt. Sometimes there is a roughness to the world that only a dad can smooth out.

I could never have imagined that I would have to wait until I was the grandfather of four, and he the great-grandfather of eight, for him to attend one of my sports events. And I certainly couldn't have known that his showing up at one would still matter to me and would feel so good. I guess the desire and need for paternal support and approval is so strong that it trumps reasonable evidence that such support may not be forthcoming. Even when submerged, the longing remains intense.

While the biological act of fathering entails no real commitment, the ongoing process of **daddying** requires a lifelong commitment to your children. But it's never too late to begin the process of becoming the father you want to be, the one you always wished you had.

—ALLAN SHEDLIN JR., Chevy Chase, MD,
parenting coach, son of Allan Shedlin,
businessman (1915–2002)

THE LISTENER

The image of a father and son lying in bed and sharing confidences is a welcome antidote to the pains of adolescence.

My dad was a milkman who got up five days a week at 3 A.M. He would drive from Brooklyn, where we lived, to the plant in the Bronx, and then to the Upper East Side of Manhattan to deliver milk.

Because he had to get up in the middle of the night, my father was usually in bed by eight. On Monday nights, my mom would go out to play cards "with the girls." When she was gone, I would go into my parents' room and ask Dad if I could speak with him. He always said yes, and we would lie there in his bed as I poured my heart out to him—often about being teased by other kids. He was completely supportive. On any number of occasions, he explained that the torment and embarrassment I was feeling as an adolescent would pass, and that the healthy thing was to let it go and not act on my anger. It was good advice but, more important, he was telling me these things when he was utterly exhausted.

When Mom came home from her evening

out, she'd have a fit that Dad was still up. But I will always remember that Dad felt that talking with me was even more important than his rest. He was always there—with advice, an encouraging word, or just a grip of his strong, rough hands.

—IRA M. GARVIN, Oakdale, NY,
retired teacher, son of Leo M. Garvin,
milkman (1913–1967)

THE ANNOUNCEMENT

When a father isn't careful, his pride can lead to his daughter's embarrassment. When a father is fortunate, his daughter forgives him.

I was the first college graduate in our family. A few years later, in a solemn ceremony, I was sworn into the bar as a lawyer in the great Maryland Court of Appeals building. As my name was called, my father stood and said, in a loud, strong voice, **"That is my daughter!"** I was mortified.

Years earlier, while sitting at his knee every Saturday night as we watched **Perry Mason,** I had proudly announced (at the age of seven) that I was going to be a lawyer. This was not only my goal, it was obviously a dream fulfilled for him too. How I wish I could hear that voice today!

—ELVIRA M. WHITE, Princess Anne, MD,
law professor, daughter of
Olden M. White, railroad worker,
steam engineer (1911–1986)

THE ALLY

A rare breed—the dad who could hear a problem without needing to solve it.

Teenagers often struggle to get along with their parents, and my mother was the one I struggled with. Neither of us seemed to be able to understand the other or communicate effectively. When things got especially hard, I would climb into the cab of my dad's pickup truck or the front seat of the car, and we would sit in the driveway and talk. I would tell him how tough things were going from my perspective, and he simply listened without taking sides. That in itself is pretty remarkable. As

I learned later on, men typically try to fix problems rather than listen to them.

But my dad was a great listener, which helped me immensely. He listened until I had shed all my tears and expressed all my feelings, even though it must have been hard for him to hear the emotional ups and downs of a teenage girl who wasn't getting along with his wife. Although he worked long hours, when I needed him, he was always there.

—**BONNIE J. MORRIS, Coon Rapids, MN,
medical transcriptionist,
daughter of Paul W. Wojahn,
retired game warden (1921)**

Loss

**"Hell to get old—
but hell not to."**
—Thomas A.
O'Halleran,
father of Linda Nitz

I didn't expect that my introduction to this section would be so personal, but on August 14, 2005, after a short but difficult battle with cancer, my mother died. A couple of weeks later, an old friend, after expressing her sympathy, said to me that one of the hardest parts of losing a parent is realizing that you are no longer a child. How right she was. For fifty-five years I had my mom to care for and comfort me. When she left us, it felt as if an enormous part of my earlier life left with her. It's hard to remember that things are different; I still find myself reaching for the phone to call her. Friends who have lost a parent tell me this impulse may never entirely go away.

Losing a parent forces us to face our own mortality, to face the fact that **we** are now the older generation. And it serves as a dramatic reminder that we too will not be here forever, and that we owe it to both our parents and our children to be the best parents we possibly can during our days on this earth. For me, at least, this reminder of mortality also reinforces the idea that we owe it to our children to let them remain our children for as long as possible. We are obligated, therefore, to take care of ourselves and attend to our health. The solemn facts of life, and the painful knowledge that it will end, remind us that time is precious.

I hadn't planned on speaking at Mom's funeral, but my sisters were overcome with grief and couldn't imagine getting up in front of the congregation and making a speech. B.A., my oldest sister, said, "Tim, would you do it? This is what you do."

I knew what she meant, but this **wasn't** something I do, or had ever done, or had even imagined doing. But I had to do it, so I asked each sister to tell me about a memory of Mom, and I agreed to serve as the vehicle for their love as well as my own.

Because we had known that Mom was dying, we, her four children, were often at her bedside. I had never seen a person die before. It was devastating to watch the process unfold, but it was healing, too, in its way. When she finally left us, we took comfort in the knowledge that she was going to a better, more peaceful place.

Near the end, when Mom took a turn for

the worse, Kathy called and told me to get to Buffalo as soon as I could. When I arrived at the hospital, her kidneys had stopped functioning and her heart was failing. "She's heavily sedated," the doctor said, "and I don't think she'll know you." I went into her room and sat by her bed. I said, "Mom, it's Tim. Mom, it's Tim." When I was a boy, she used to wake me in the morning by standing at the bottom of the stairs and softly speaking my name; that was all I needed to start the day. That night, I found myself using that same voice, with that same inflection. And she heard me. Suddenly she opened her eyes, grabbed my hand, and squeezed it. Then she drifted off again.

Time was running out. B.A. and Kathy were with me in Mom's hospital room, but Trish, our youngest sister, had just moved to Florida. At two in the morning I called her and said, "You have to get here." Later that morning, she came into the room and immediately started rubbing Mom's forehead. "Mom, it's Trishy," she said. Mom opened an eye and acknowledged her youngest child with a big tear. A few hours later, Mom's life was over.

My parents had always taught us that it's important to be there for people who are suffering a loss, and now we learned how true that really was. Sister Lucille, my eighth-grade teacher, flew in to be with us, bringing with her a small squadron of nuns, who were enormously comforting. Friends and neighbors came to visit, and, to our surprise, so did the milkman who had delivered milk to our house fifty years earlier. My sisters and I, who had sent out so many cards and letters to other grieving families over the years, got to experience the comfort and compassion that the daily mail can bring. The many phone calls, the deliveries of food—all of it helped us cope with Mom's loss.

During this period, more than one person shared with us the insightful words of Colin Murray Parkes, a British psychiatrist and author. **Grief,** he wrote, **is the price we pay for love.**

THE FAN

Most of us hope that our dad will always be at the other end of the line.

My dad was an ardent Yankees fan. My mom told me that when they were "keeping company," she would pack a big lunch for him and he would get lost at Yankee Stadium for a Sunday doubleheader. He'd stay the whole day, from batting practice to the last out of the second game.

When we couldn't get to the stadium, we listened to Red Barber and Mel Allen broadcast the games on the old Philco radio. Or, when it was working, we'd watch the games on our old thirteen-inch black-and-white TV. I'd pull his easy chair into place and get his slippers ready. Right after dinner we'd take our positions in front of the TV: Dad in his chair and me at his feet, learning the fine points of the game.

In the fall of 1955 I was back at school in

the Bronx. One September morning, a monitor came to my classroom with a note instructing me to report to the principal's office with my coat and books. My father was there in a shirt and tie, leaning over the principal's desk. She was a stern woman who believed that discipline was the core of learning. I remember her telling my dad that he could not take me out of class that day unless it was a matter of life or death. He looked her in the eye and said, "The Yankees are playing the Brooklyn Dodgers. It's the seventh game of the World Series. It **is** a matter of life or death."

Somehow, my dad had scored two tickets to the game. He could have called anyone to go with him—a friend, a good customer, even my mom—but he came to school, stole me away, and spent that fall afternoon with his son at Yankee Stadium.

Fast-forward nearly twenty years to a Saturday afternoon. The Yankees are on TV and it's Old Timers' Day. They're playing the Cleveland Indians. There's the obligatory two-inning game prior to the real game, matching some of the Yankees from the fifties and sixties against some of the Indians from the same era. The Yankee Clipper was in the stands; he stood and waved. Yogi, Bobby Richardson, and all the guys were there. This was the team my dad had taught me about. This was the glue that bonded us together.

I grabbed the phone and dialed my parents' number. Mom picked up the phone, and as soon as I heard her voice, I was jolted back to reality. What was I thinking? Dad had died almost ten years ago, and I had completely forgotten. I made some small talk with Mom, told her about the game, and hung up. I watched those two innings, laughing and crying at the same time.

—ARNOLD ANNUNZIATA, Las Vegas, NV,
sales manager, son of
Frank Annunziata, butcher
(1910–1953)

THE PATIENT

Sometimes you just have to say it—even when the other person knows.

When my father suffered a stroke and was taken to the hospital, my life seemed to dissolve as I realized I had never told him that I loved him. I was terrified that he might not know. I got in my car and drove to the hospital, not knowing if I would find him alive or dead. The hospital was overcrowded and he was lying on a gurney in the hall. When I saw his face, I dissolved into tears and threw myself on him, saying, "I love you, Dad, I've always loved you!" He was weak and very surprised. I felt his arms come up and embrace me as he whispered in my ear, "And I always knew."

—JUDITH BRADY CLUTE,
Forest Knolls, CA, retired,
daughter of Owen Brady, fireman,
policeman (1895–1985)

THE STRENGTH

A father's strength gave courage to his son. He would need it.

On a summer morning in 1971, when I was seven and the oldest of four siblings, my father gathered us into the family room for a meeting. Amid tears and grief, he explained that our mother, who had been sick for some time with cancer, had died last night in the hospital.

Dad said there would be changes we would have to face, and we would need to stick together as a family. I remember looking at this broken man, telling us with great conviction that while life would not be easy, we would all pull together and get through this as a family. Even through his brokenness, I could feel Dad's strength.

Over the years, Dad's vision was true. He owned a small nursery business with his brothers, and he provided a great example of courage just by getting us out of bed every morning, getting us off to school, providing us with dinner, and putting us to bed. He believed that you should never feel sorry for yourself or your situation. He warned me repeatedly that other people would want to feel sorry for us, but that we shouldn't let it take root. We would never be allowed to use our family tragedy as an excuse for anything.

Mom's death gave me the opportunity to have a special relationship with my father. Through the years, as the typical accomplishments came to pass—Little League, Boy Scouts, graduations, and all the rest—there was always a mixture of joy and grief. Dad and I connected on an emotional level that was special.

I always looked forward to the day my dad would see his grandchildren. Unfortunately he died before that could happen. That moment in my life was challenging, yet I felt so blessed to have a father like I had.

A few years ago, my five-year-old son died suddenly of an illness. Words cannot describe what I felt. Suddenly, I was faced with a similar situation. I too had my moment in the family room, broken and explaining as best I could to my other children what had happened. In the depths of my own grief, I could feel and hear my father's encouragement as, "Take one more step, one more step." These words were not empty, as I could (and still do) stand on his shoulders and draw strength from his example of courage and perseverance over the years of raising a family as a single man. Life is not always easy, but it is still good. Thanks, Dad.

—BILL DeSisto, Orono, ME,
professor, son of Joseph "Bill" DeSisto,
nursery owner (1933–1994)

THE FIREMAN

Her dad was a little removed. Sometimes, it turns out, there is a reason.

Stash, as my father was known, was a firefighter—and more. When he worked night or afternoon shifts, he also worked by day as a house-painter. He had his first heart attack in his forties but never learned to slow down. He worked tenaciously to provide for us.

Because of his countless hours on the job, we almost never spent quality time with him. Sometimes he took us fishing, but although he was physically present, he was far away in his thoughts. When I helped him in the garden we would talk about composting, but we barely knew each other.

Years later, when I was married with children, he spent six months recovering at our house after surgery, and we finally had some quality time together. At my kitchen table, I met a man who was very different from the father I had known. The robust, invincible firefighter was now frail and legally blind. At first we talked about nothing in particular, but gradually the conversation became more personal. To my astonishment, I learned that my father had quit school in sixth grade because his father used to beat him for bringing home books. "Bad enough you waste all day there!" he would say. "You will not bring books in here." I learned about his childhood during the Depression, how his father was out of work, which left the children responsible for putting food on the table. At one point, my father's job was to walk along the railroad tracks and collect pieces of coal that had fallen from passing trains, which he would bring home to provide heat for the family.

But the most amazing thing I learned was that there was a reason we had never been close: My father had done this deliberately! Knowing the dangers he faced as a firefighter, he had decided many years earlier to keep a certain distance from his family, so if he ever died in the line of duty we wouldn't grieve too much. I had a lot of trouble processing that, but after several sleepless nights I understood that he had lived a life of dignity. He never complained. He held his head high and met each obstacle in his path. He worked hard until he could work no longer.

Of course my father was mistaken. His theory of staying apart to lessen the grieving? It didn't work. When he died, I mourned the loss of the man I had almost never known.

—**CINDY DUNCAN, Southborough, MA, respiratory therapist, daughter of Stanley J. Samsel, firefighter (1918–1998)**

THE HAPPY MAN

Dad left her, but he left her feeling fortunate.

My father was a happy man. He was born in 1925 in tiny Lena, Illinois, the eighth and last child of Italian immigrants.

His focus was our family, and everything he did revolved around us. He went into business for himself, leaving a steady paycheck to be better able to provide for us. Mom couldn't drive, so Dad became our chauffeur. Thinking back, I realize how we took that for granted. Dad drove long hours for his business as a manufacturer's representative and then cheerfully drove us to our activities. We all cherished that car time with him. We had some great talks in the car and some great laughs.

Dinner was sacred family time. My father, a true Italian, loved to eat, and Mom was a great cook. I can hear his sigh of satisfaction as he pushed back his chair and put his napkin on the table. "Kids," he'd say, "you can't get food like that on the outside!"

Dad's love for Mom, and hers for him, was very comforting as we were growing up. I remember them holding hands, stealing a kiss in the kitchen, and looking at each other across the table as if they shared a special and wonderful secret. When my sisters and I would tell our fortunes, we'd make up lists of possible cities we'd live in, how many children we'd have, and the qualities of our future husbands. "Like Daddy" was always on the list.

He treated all of us with respect and instilled in us a sense of possibility. He encouraged us with, "You never know unless you try." He was an optimist who liked to remind us that it takes more muscles to frown than it does to smile. He was a happy man.

When Dad was in his fifties, we realized that something was terribly wrong. He would ask the same question over and over, and repeat the same remark. Dad, who prided himself on his memory, forgot to submit orders. Dad, who had an uncanny sense of direction, became confused when driving to familiar places. After much testing, we were devastated to learn the diagnosis: Alzheimer's. As the reality sank in, I asked him how he was coping. My father, whose Catholic faith was as strong as his love of family, replied, "Well, honey, if this is what the Good Lord wants of me, then I accept it."

During one family gathering, every moment of forgetfulness was like a knife in my heart. I was pregnant with my fifth child and acutely aware that she would never know her wonderful grandfather. I went to lie down and be alone for a while. After a few minutes, Dad passed by and saw me. "Honey, it's cold in here. Let me get you a blanket." That one moment, that simple act of love as my father tenderly tucked that blanket around me, summed up the essence of the special man he was.

Too soon, the light faded from his remarkable blue eyes. With great love, dignity, and courage, Mom took care of Dad at home for the fifteen years of his illness. We were all with him at the end and sent him to the Good Lord with, "We love you, Daddy."

Before his illness, my father taught me the freeing power of unconditional love, the confidence to believe in myself, appreciation of our beautiful world, and the benefits of approaching life positively. After his illness, my father taught me the freeing power of unconditional love, the wisdom to accept what I cannot change, and the knowledge that faith and strength can come from suffering, as fire hones steel.

My father was a happy man. I am a lucky woman.

—JUDITH ANN MCCANSE,
Rockford, IL, speech pathologist,
daughter of Jack P. Bonavia,
manufacturer's representative
(1925–1997)

THE WORSHIPER

It was a private moment, but his kids all knew. Maybe it was best that way.

My dad was born in 1915 in Worcester, Massachusetts, and left this world in 1996 in that same city. He was the husband of Clara, "that girl in the red dress" from the USO dance. They were married for fifty-two years and had six children, whom my father considered his greatest work.

After getting out of the navy following World War II, he worked as a metallurgist for most of his life. It was a job he did not especially love, but it was steady work and provided food on the table, parochial schooling, and college educations for the six of us. He lived and died a simple life: God was first, Mom a close second, and his children not far behind.

My dad died a beautiful death, surrounded by his family, who loved him and one another without reservation. He was diagnosed with cancer in May and died in September. I am the lone child who moved far from home, but my sister and four brothers were wonderful, helping our parents with doctor appointments, shopping, and loving care until Dad was hospitalized a week before his death. I got to spend a long weekend with him, and he promised me a second date when I returned with my husband the following weekend. That second date was replaced by a thirty-six-hour vigil at his bedside—reminiscing, laughing, and crying. During that time, we all shared a similar story but from differing vantage points.

My dad had a rocking chair in the kitchen, near the only TV in the house. This was where he read the paper after work, where he talked to each of us about our day at school, and where he took a nap after supper even though he claimed he wasn't sleeping. While sitting around his hospital bed, I mentioned that I had seen Dad kneeling at his chair at night and praying just before he turned off the lights and went to bed. During the spring and fall months, when the glass door was in place instead of the screen, I could see his reflection through my bedroom door. His head was bowed down in his hands and he was kneeling on the linoleum floor, solemn, quiet, and, from my perspective as a little girl, holy.

After I said this, one of my brothers said that on nights when he didn't fall right to sleep, he had a perfect view of our dad from his bottom bunk in the room that my four brothers shared. He too recalled seeing Dad on his knees in prayer—a memory that had stayed with him all these years. One by one, my siblings shared their own memories of Dad praying at his chair. It could have been during a trip to the bathroom, which was off the kitchen, or a top-bunk view from the boys' bedroom, or a memory from one of the older ones, who got to stay up on the weekends and decided to raid the fridge while watching late-night movies. In each case, it was the same sight: Dad kneeling and praying at his chair.

For some reason, each of us had thought we were the only one who ever saw Dad doing this. And for each of us, the sight of this man humbling himself before God, and very likely praying on our behalf, was a cherished memory.

Maybe it was because Dad looked so comfortable at prayer. Maybe it was because we each knew it was his time for peace and quiet. Maybe it was because it seemed like such a personal time for him that none of us wanted to invade it. This shared memory seemed to be a fitting tribute to a loving father who had taught us so much about faith by the way he had lived his life. Even in his death, he was still sharing that faith-filled life with each of us.

The man who had always told my mom that he loved her more than he loved himself may have left us physically, but not without leaving an indelible mark on our hearts. It was a beautiful way to die.

—JULIE MILLER, Ottawa Lake, MI,
pediatric physiatrist,
daughter of Jeremiah Gerard Foley,
metallurgist (1915–1996)

THE MEMORY

Mind and memory, working together.

My father is so optimistic that anything cloudy doesn't seem to penetrate. But when I was eight years old, his father died—my beloved grandfather. My father was not a religious man, but every morning he went to the synagogue to say kaddish for his father. Once, when I was with him, I asked him why he was crying.

"I miss your grandfather," he said.

"I miss him too."

"You know," he said, "if you try very hard, and you really imagine, you can get him back." And I did. I could get more time with my grandfather! That was the beginning of my religious life, the first step in my becoming a rabbi.

—**MICHAEL PALEY**, New York, NY,
rabbi, son of Bertram Paley,
clothing manufacturer
(1927)

THE STORIES

Comforting words for difficult times.

My dad had a private law practice until he was eighty-three. His last year at the office was his most lucrative as an attorney, and he remained a vital, engaged man until a disease without a name that combined the worst elements of Parkinson's and Alzheimer's took hold of him.

I wouldn't wish what happened next on any family. We watched him pass rapidly down the staircase of this illness until the man who couldn't do enough for other people couldn't do a damn 'thing for anyone, especially himself. I remember feeling a weird, wistful happiness one morning as I fed him some breakfast, thinking that for the first time in my life I could do something important for him. That happy feeling was short lived.

He passed in and out of mental fogs. Repeated viewings of **Witness for the Prosecution** seemed to keep his attention. One day, after months without talking clearly, he said one understandable sentence to my brother: "Take care of your mother." He died a few months later, about three years after the illness struck.

During the time he was ill, I remember feeling so sure that this was how we'd remember him—sick. Before the Parkinson's made him bedridden, his behavior was unpredictable, and we didn't leave any of the grandkids alone with him. The day I took his car keys away, he told me to take my damn kids, get out of the house, and never come back. I knew that wasn't my father talking. The man who couldn't figure out how to put on a pullover sweater wasn't him either. But I was heartsick.

I want to reassure other sons and daughters who are in this position or who might be someday: You won't remember these bad patches very clearly after your dad or mom is gone. You'll even have difficulty remembering the names of people you thought you'd never forget, like a saintly home health aide or a particularly kind doctor. You won't believe this while you're in the midst of it, but it's true.

Instead, you'll look at old pictures, and of course you'll tell stories. If your family is Irish, the stories start at the wake. The stories heal. The stories keep him close.

—MARY DESMOND PINKOWISH,
Larchmont, NY, medical writer,
daughter of John F. Desmond,
lawyer (1912–1998)

THE END

A memorable send-off for a special man.

My father taught me that nobody is perfect, that you become ugly when you hold a grudge, that you must always be willing to laugh at yourself, and that, when all is said and done, everything boils down to family. How great a man he must have been for my mom to have crawled into his hospital bed when he was dying and not get up until he knew that she would love him forever. And when he knew that, he finally let go.

—LORRI ROTHGEB-MAS, Reston, VA,
administrative assistant,
daughter of Paul Maynard Rothgeb,
retired banker (1928–2003)

THE BLURT

Anyone who has lost their dad will know exactly what he's talking about.

When my father died, I cried so hard while writing the eulogy that I was afraid of shorting out the computer keyboard. At the funeral it took every bit of emotional strength I had to get through the service. I supported my mom as she kissed Dad's body for the last time, and as she went up and later down the long aisle at our home church—the same aisle she had walked as a happy bride in 1949. It was appropriate: Dad went to his grave wearing the shoes he was married in. They felt good, he said, wearing them often in what turned out to be his final days.

Special guests? Those guys from the offtrack betting parlor who were his pals in his postretirement years. I almost expected a chorus of "Can Do," the pari-mutuel paean from **Guys and Dolls.** By the time I got to the ending of the seventy-seven-years-in-seven-minutes tribute, in which I described a heavenly reunion with Dad's beloved parents and his seven deceased siblings, my voice had more cracks than a stale Christmas cookie.

The trip to the cemetery was almost anticlimactic. The mourners gathered in a chapel, the last prayers were uttered, and we all headed off to the funeral breakfast.

And that is where I almost blew it.

We were passing the platters of kielbasa (both fresh and smoked), mashed potatoes, peas and carrots, and chicken when I took note of who was sitting with whom at the ten long tables at the restaurant. Then I almost blurted out words that had seemed natural for all my forty-eight years. What spurred it I cannot explain, and I truly thank God I stopped before they hit my tongue.

The blurt?
Where's Dad?

—John Smyntek, Detroit, MI,
editor, columnist,
son of John E. Smyntek,
meat packer (1921–1998)

MR. PERFECT

Sometimes an innocuous comment, repeated often enough, can take on great meaning. Sometimes it can even define a life.

We often talk about my father's two favorite comments, which were simple but powerful. A nice dinner, a funny conversation, or a beautiful day at the lake would prompt, "Are we lucky, or what?" Those words had a tremendous impact—seeping into my soul, centering my priorities, and reminding me that we are all very fortunate, despite the difficulties we may face.

His other favorite was, "It's perfect; I wouldn't change a thing." We rarely hear the word **perfect,** especially from our parents, so when he viewed perfection we were showered with the sweetest contentment.

His words still resonate for me, and in those moments all is still right with the world. On good days I hold on to his life, well lived. On bad days I mourn our loss and try to remember that our time here is finite, but life remains eternal. The loss can be crushing at times, but the pain is eased when I hear him speaking to my soul, reminding me that all is well.

The ultimate goal of our journey is to fill life with love. My father's journey overflowed with love. Was he lucky, or what? Dad, you were perfect. I wouldn't change a thing.

—KATE RANKIN DALTON, Fairport, NY, mom, daughter of Richard W. Rankin, electrical engineer (1926–2003)

Baseball

"My father, who saved
nothing for sentimental
reasons, had decided to
save this, a keepsake of
our afternoon together
at the ballpark."

—EDWIN ROMOND,
son of Edwin Romond

On the evening of April 14, 2005, I had an experience that most baseball fans can only dream about—the opportunity to attend the very first game in the history of my (new) home team. After a thirty-four-year absence, major league baseball had returned to Washington, D.C.

When I was a boy, my annual birthday present was a trip to Cleveland with my dad. Cleveland was the closest major-league city to Buffalo, and we would drive to a doubleheader between the Indians and the Yankees, my favorite team, where I could watch Yogi Berra, my favorite player. These trips were always the high point of my year.

As an adult, when I lived in New York, I took my newborn son to Yankee Stadium, hoping, I guess, that the sights and sounds of baseball would be imprinted on his tender mind. It must have worked, because when we moved to Washington, Luke and I often went to Orioles games. And now, finally, we had our own team, the Nationals, playing just a few minutes away at RFK Memorial Stadium—where the old Washington Senators used to play.

Luke arrived home from college in time for opening night. There was a huge crowd, a complete sellout. It took a while to get into the stadium, because the president was going to throw out the first pitch. But as the fans stood in line to go through the metal detectors, I saw excitement and anticipation in their eyes rather than impatience. People were so **happy** that baseball was back. Looking around, I noticed a great many dads holding hands with their sons and their daughters, and for a moment I was back in Cleveland, eight years old, holding Dad's hand as we entered cavernous Municipal Stadium.

Luke and I took our seats behind the third-base dugout. In a beautiful moment before the game began, some of the former Washington Senators, including Mickey Vernon, Roy Sievers, and Frank Howard, took the field and stood at their old positions. Then, in a moment that gave me chills, the Washington Nationals came out and took their places next to the veterans. The older men handed their gloves to the younger ones and left the field to a rousing reception.

After a tribute to our troops, President Bush

came out in a Washington Nationals jacket. His staff had let it slip that he had been practicing for a couple of weeks, and with the same ball that had been used in the final Washington Senators home game in 1971, he threw out the first pitch—high and inside. Then he walked off the mound and headed for the third-base dugout.

Just before he went in, he spotted Luke and me and yelled, "Nice seats, Russert!" For that moment, it seemed to me, he had slipped back into his former incarnation as the owner of the Texas Rangers—the very team, as it happened, that had taken over the old Washington franchise.

I went to a number of Nationals' games during their first season, including one with my NBC colleague Steve Capus, who brought his son, Max. A few days later, Steve sent me a note of thanks for sharing the tickets, and the words he wrote went right to my heart. "A baseball stadium through a child's eyes is about as good as it gets, with the green green grass that goes on forever. What a day—with Max and a good friend watching a great pastime. Sitting with your son inside a ballpark is almost a religious experience."

I still feel that way.

THE TICKET

Sometimes the tiniest piece of paper can hold a very big memory.

My father shocked our neighbors one day when he stood at our attic window and tossed out family heirlooms for the garbage. He wasn't sentimental about material goods. In fact, I don't recall that he ever saved anything for the sake of nostalgia—except once. It had to do with a baseball game in October.

I was the only one in my family who cared about baseball. Because we had only one television in our house, I usually listened to Yankee games on the radio while dreaming that someday I would actually watch my heroes in person at Yankee Stadium.

That winter, I wrote away for a schedule and unfolded it every night, gazed at the summer dates, and dreamed. To my surprise, one evening I saw my father examining it before going out to load his truck.

The following Sunday, he was shaving at the kitchen sink before church. Because he was a truck driver, he kept change in a red money bag to prevent coins from falling out of his pockets. As he lathered his face, he turned to me and said, "Take some silver from my bag and put it in a jar. Each week we'll add to it, and maybe we can go to Yankee Stadium this summer."

I immediately washed out a peanut butter jar and attached a label: YANKEE STADIUM FUND, 1960.

Each of us contributed to the jar weekly, and by midsummer it was stuffed with money. By the end of August, however, we still hadn't gone to a game because my father had had to work every Saturday and even some Sundays. As I followed the Yankees' pennant drive into September, I hid a growing fear that we wouldn't get to a game that season.

One evening, while helping my father load his truck, I informed him that there were only two more weekends when the Yankees would be playing at home.

He took off his cap and said, "Well, don't worry, Edwin. Things are sure to slow down and we'll have a free Saturday."

We walked home with the chill of autumn

reminding us that the time for baseball was running out.

The night before the next-to-last game of the season, my father said, "I have to go to Trenton, but if I don't have to make extra deliveries, I should be home by eleven. That is, if you still want to go."

The next morning I sat waiting. Soon it was eleven-fifteen with no sign of my father. I continued to sit, holding our money jar and trying not to notice that it was now eleven-fifty. I struggled to accept still another year of waiting when the door crashed open and my father yelled, "Give me five minutes to change. We're going!"

It looked like a medieval castle with the giant letters YANKEE STADIUM. I could barely breathe after my father bought two blue ticket strips and we filed up three flights of ramps and finally out the runway to the upper deck.

It was even more magnificent than I had imagined: thousands of seats, emerald grass and, best of all, no longer on a scrapbook page but there in person, my New York Yankees!

I sat cheering every pitch, but for my father it must have been a long afternoon trying to follow a game he didn't understand. (He just wasn't a sports fan.) Several times I paused in my rapture to look at him, his huge frame jammed into the seat, his face lined with fatigue from working all Saturday morning after working all week. I wish I could remember that I expressed my gratitude as we sat there, father and son, watching a summer game in the autumn sunshine.

After the game we rode home past all the Jersey towns my father had driven through over twenty-five years of delivering freight. When we got home, my father said, "Save that jar. We'll start putting money in tomorrow for our next game." Immediately I taped on a new label: YANKEE STADIUM FUND, 1961.

We would go to two more games together.

On the second day of 1963, when I was in eighth grade, my father died suddenly while changing a truck tire. I threw away the jar.

After his funeral, our house was filled with neighbors and relatives, but I didn't want to talk with anybody. I had never in my life felt so empty. I walked upstairs to my parents' bedroom, hoping, I suppose, to find some comfort from seeing what was his. The high-top work shoes, his black speckled cap, even his red money bag were all there in quiet dignity. Then I noticed his old prayer book lying on the dresser. As I slowly thumbed through the yellowed pages, something blue fell out and floated to the floor. I picked up the faded ticket stub and read, **October 1, 1960, General Admission.** My father, who saved nothing for sentimental reasons, had decided to save this, a keepsake of our afternoon together at the ballpark. Carefully, I placed the ticket stub back into his prayer book, as if it were something sacred, and slowly walked downstairs to begin the rest of my life without him.

—EDWIN ROMOND, Wind Gap, PA,
poet, son of Edwin Romond,
truck driver (1909–1963)

THE BALL

A visitor from another planet might eventually come to understand the infield fly rule, but could he ever grasp the thrill of watching your dad chasing down a foul ball?

One night, when I was seven or eight, my dad (a former Minor League pitcher for the South Phillies) took me to a ball game in Shibe Park in Philadelphia. The wooden seats had just been painted red, and they were still a bit sticky. In the fourth inning, a foul ball came into our section in the upper level along first base. This was the closest I had ever been to a real baseball. There was mass chaos as a multitude of bodies dove for the ball, which caromed off a seat before it disappeared. Because nobody emerged with it, I asked Dad what had happened. "Wow, that was close," he said.

That night, I went in to kiss him good night and to thank him for taking me to the game. When I came back, I noticed a lump in my pillow. Under it was a Major League baseball—with a streak of red paint on it.

—MARK FELDMAN, Dallas, TX,
physician, son of Jerome Feldman,
accountant (1921–1989)

THE YANKEE

Father, daughter, beer, and baseball. Is there anything better?

It was Friday, July 3, 1953, and the Fourth of July weekend was about to begin. I was turning eight on the fifth, and I thought the colorful exploding light show was to celebrate my special day. My dad had told me that, and dads didn't make things up.

In June he had taken me across the river from Leonia, New Jersey, to Yankee Stadium, with the promise of more visits later in the summer. He laughed when I imitated the vendors, yelling "Be-ah he-ah!"—**Beer here!** At home, Mel Allen's soft southern voice calling the games from our black-and-white TV had taught me that baseball and Ballantine were part of a northern New Jersey summer.

I went out to play that Friday with the understanding that I would return for lunch when I heard Mom's familiar midday whistle. But noontime came and went, so, hot and hungry, I hurried up the block to our house. There, in front, was a big white station wagon with a red light on top. Our neighbor, Mrs. Izzo, guided me gently into her house. I watched my mother get into the white car along with a stretcher that carried my dad, and then watched it drive away. At forty-five, my father had suffered a stroke and was on his way to the hospital. There would be no picnic, no fireworks, and no birthday cake that year.

My dad came home in August, unable to walk, his left arm hanging limply at his side.

But he was still devoted to the Yankees, so with much difficulty, my short little mother propped him into his favorite wingback chair, where he sat for hours watching his beloved team.

I quickly realized that if I wanted to spend time with him, I'd have to sit with him, so I did. Together we watched the rest of the 1953 baseball season play out. He managed the team from his chair, explaining every stat and tactic to me, and I knew we were sharing something special. I watched the fabric on the back of the chair turn dark from the oil in his hair. He laughed out loud when I said I wanted to marry Whitey Ford and told me I'd better check with Mrs. Ford. I thought he meant Whitey's mother.

Labor Day came and school started. I raced home each day to watch the Yankees win the pennant and play in the World Series against the Brooklyn Dodgers. The Yankees won in six games, the autumn leaves turned to flame, and the summer of 1953 disappeared.

I shared four more seasons at my dad's side, until he died suddenly in the spring of 1958, when I was twelve. I still have Daddy's wingback chair, and whenever I see anything with a Yankees logo, something pulls at my heart. It could be my dad, telling me that when we meet again I should bring his chair and, if I can find one, an ice-cold bottle of Ballantine beer.

—DIANE COLE MATHIS,
DeLeon Springs, FL, travel agent,
daughter of Raymond Garfield Cole,
salesman (1908–1958)

THE QUIZ

BASEBALL TRIVIA HELPS SAVE NATION!

My father enlisted in the U.S. Navy in 1943 and was assigned to the USS **Hinsdale,** an attack transport, where he was put in charge of landing craft to take troops ashore. He landed marines at Iwo Jima and Okinawa.

At Okinawa they were hit by a kamikaze plane. It wasn't a direct hit, and although seven men were lost, the ship survived. Two days later, they were clearing out the wreckage—I still have a bracelet made from a piece of one of the wings—when a huge undetonated bomb was discovered. They roused my father at 2 A.M. and told him to take a boat to a ship that had a demolition expert and bring him back to defuse the bomb.

As he approached the ship, he was asked for the authentication code. But the code was changed daily, and having just been awakened at 0200 hours, he didn't have that day's code. There was an awkward moment. Suddenly, questions started flying at him. What Major League teams are based in New York? Who played in the World Series last year? What is a shutout? Where is the Hall of Fame located? Who is known as the Yankee Clipper?

My father gave them all the right answers, and they decided that anyone who knew that much about baseball had to be a true-blue American. The demolition expert went back with him and defused what turned out to be a five-hundred-plus-pound bomb. Joe DiMaggio never knew the full extent of his contribution to the war.

—MARI-JO WOOLFE, Tucson, AZ, teacher, daughter of Joseph M. Decker, real estate broker (1907–1988)

Forgiveness

"Learn to love
people for who they
are and forgive
them for who they
are not."
—ERNEST B.
RUSSELL SR.,
father of Jay Russell

Maybe I'm naïve, but I never expected that this book would include a chapter on forgiveness. I had a few arguments with my dad over the years, especially when I was in college, but they usually ended within a couple of hours. Early on, I would fight with my father from time to time. "I'm going to run away," I told him when I was eleven. His response? "Make sure you pack your gloves, because it's cold out there." Another time, when I threatened to leave home, he said, "Fine. Don't let the door hit you in the ass on the way out."

I was startled. Was he encouraging me to leave? Whatever he meant, exactly, his use of a bad word in those more innocent times made me giggle, which lessened the intensity of the moment and may well have been his intention. From time to time I was grounded, reprimanded, or punished, but there was always an unbreakable bond and a path to reconciliation.

Growing up Catholic, I was taught repeatedly about the importance of forgiveness and repentance. **Forgive us our trespasses,** the Our Father says, **as we forgive those who trespass against us.** But it was never really necessary to apply that idea to my own family, and it never occurred to me that some people might have to. The fact that a father and his son or daughter might go through an extended period of not speaking to each other lay outside of my experience. I know it happens, of course; people have told me that they haven't spoken to their father for twenty years, or that a big argument decades ago was never resolved. As I read the letters that came in, which included a few stories of this type, I realized how fortunate I was that none of this sounded familiar. I also realized I ought to include a chapter on forgiveness, about healing some of the ruptures that do occur, from time to time, between fathers and their children.

Quite unexpectedly, I may have played a role in one of these reconciliations. During my book tour for **Big Russ & Me,** a woman in St. Louis asked me to sign two books—one for her husband, the other for her son. "I'm giving a copy to each one," she said, "and I hope my son will call home now."

Later, she sent me a brief note: "I just

wanted to let you know that my son **did** call home."

That was it, nothing more. I don't know what caused the break or exactly what healed it. But her letter meant the world to me.

Sometimes, as the letters in this chapter make clear, the rift between father and child is deep, painful, and long lasting. And sometimes it just seems that way. On Capitol Hill, not long ago, a man came up to me to thank me for writing a book about my dad. "After I read it," he said, "I understood my old man differently. He rarely talked to me over the years, and I always thought he didn't like me. I understood his silence as disdain, until I read that your father was also silent, and yet you love each other very much." He went on to say that he reached out to his dad, who just needed someone to jump-start their relationship. "My dad is still pretty quiet," he told me, "but now we are really enjoying each other's company."

So often, even when the rift seems insurmountable, all it requires is for one person to take the first step. More often than not, the other person is relieved—and is more than willing to reciprocate.

THE MONSTER

Affection delayed is not always affection denied.

He sounds old and his voice is tired. It's been fifteen years since I've heard it, but it's definitely him.

I am caught in that melodramatic made-for-television moment where I learn that my estranged father is dying of brain cancer and I have only—days? weeks? months?—to "set things right" between us.

I have to laugh. I'm a writer, and I never would have dreamed up such a trite, overdone scenario. But here I am, actually living it. It gets better: I get the news about his cancer the day I am fired from my newspaper job. Has God moved to Hollywood?

My brother, Todd, calls, distraught. I am either incredibly calm or in total shock because I feel nothing—no grief, no anger, no sense of sadness. Nothing. "No one gets out of this alive," I reassure him. "We all die."

How is that reassuring? I don't know. "He was a monster," Todd says. "But he's our monster," he adds, as though that makes a difference. Maybe monsters, especially childhood ones, aren't so frightening when they're dying of brain cancer.

The childhood years of being beaten, of bleeding, of anger and shame and all the typical and not-so-typical physical, emotional, and mental abuse are distant memories now. Thanks to therapy—years of Prozac and screaming at empty chairs in my therapist's office—I reached "closure" years ago. Or so I thought. Maybe I haven't.

After our last conversation in 1991, when he told me he wished I were dead and I had never been the daughter he wanted me to be, I threatened to outlive the old bastard—excuse me, the old monster—just so I could piss on his grave. I'm surprised when my brother remembers.

"I'll stand guard for you if you still want to do that," he says sadly. I have to think about it, I reply.

Three days later I'm in the parking lot at McDonald's on a cell phone. "Hey, old man. It's your daughter—Becky," I say.

"Hey, Beck, how are you? You sound— good, real good," he says. He's in his office, working with his accountant to get his business in order so he can sell it.

"Yeah." I smile. "I'm good. Hey, I heard you had cancer."

He doesn't miss a beat. "Yeah, they diagnosed it last week."

I know, I'm thinking. I heard from your sister, who called everyone and told us.

"How bad?" I ask.

"Stage four," he says. Stage four is terminal.

"That sucks," I say matter-of-factly.

He laughs. "Yeah, it does." There is silence for a second.

"Well, you sure swung for the fences, didn't you? If you're going to have it, might as well have the worst possible kind," I tell him.

"Yeah, I guess so." He laughs again. We talk about what I'm doing now. I'm a freelance medical writer, and have been for about forty-eight hours.

He's a children's dentist. Upon hearing that I'm now doing medical research writing, he assumes I know all the medical jargon and lingo that makes up his world. He is looking for connections, for common ground. So am I.

So he launches into the medical realm of the drugs he's taking or going to take, as though he were prescribing them to a patient rather than taking them himself. He is honest about the outcome. "They're end-stage drugs," he says. We both pause.

That information out of the way, our conversation turns to photography, a passion we have both shared since he began taking photos in 1969 and that I took up shortly thereafter.

At seventy-three he is dying, but in the meantime he is learning Photoshop, as I am at forty-nine. There were moments now, I remember, when we did have some good times.

We talk cameras, digital and otherwise, megapixels and burst rates, Nikon versus Canon's latest camera—the EOS—which really kicks butt, I assure him. He likes Nikon. I begin to grieve for the losses of the past fifteen years—advice not given, requests and fears unshared. I curse Hollywood through my tears. I saw the movies, I just never got the point. Now I do, I think.

Damn. He's going to die before I win a Pulitzer. I won't get a chance to show him how well I did, that I succeeded in spite of his proclamation that I'd only "get married, get pregnant, and have babies." He'll never know

I really am the daughter he wanted. The regrets pour in.

I doubt he remembers any of the things that have haunted me for forty-plus years. Once the chemo treatments start he may not remember much of anything, let alone the past. The only "story" about my father will be what remains in my mind and in my brother's.

I tell him that I'll be coming down to see him in a week or so. We'll have lunch or dinner—if he'd like to—and we'll talk some more. He'd like that, he says.

After fifteen years, can I convince him of that in the time it takes to sit down to one dinner? I don't know if we'll even have that dinner. The chemo may prove too much.

Todd was right. After all these years he's still our monster. But now that he's dying, I say the magic words that will transform him.

"I love you, Dad."

For the first time I hear him blush. "I love you too."

And we hang up.

—BECKY BLANTON, Craig, CO,
photojournalist, daughter of
H. D. Blanton, pedodontist
(1932–2006)

THE QUESTION

A dream, a child, a question—and suddenly a door opens.

My parents separated when I was thirteen, and by the time I was sixteen I had no contact with my father. This went on for about ten years, until I had a dream in which a faceless child looked up at me and asked, "Mommy, why don't you speak to Grandpa?"

The next day I broke my silence and called my father—the best thing I ever did. It has been about seven years since we resumed our relationship, and in those years I have had three children who adore him as he adores them. I can't imagine them not having the chance to know this remarkable man I call Daddy.

What has my father taught me? Forgiveness. He answered my call that day and accepted me with open arms, and he showed me that the time we had "lost" was far less important than the many times we would share from that day on. Forgiveness—what a beautiful gift! How blessed I am, not only to have found it within myself but to have received it from him as well.

—Marla Kovatch, Flanders, NJ,
speech pathologist, daughter of
Michael S. Bailleau,
produce manager (1939)

THE SHELL GAME

I'm tempted to ask them what happened, but I'm going to accept it just the way it is.

Every birthday or Father's Day, I would buy Dad a bag of white pistachio nuts. We'd devour them together and then play tricks on each other by hiding bags of shells where the uneaten nuts used to be. How delighted he was when I fell for it and reached in to find a handful of shells! And I was delighted when I could trick him back.

The day before my twenty-fifth birthday, my father disowned me. We had a major falling-out at Disney World, where Dad and his new wife were treating us to a week's vacation. Falling-out: a strange way to describe an argument but an apt way to describe the sensation of losing one's balance, of being catapulted out of childhood into a new and more frightening vision of the world and one's place in it. We were about to head off to a dinner show, the Hoop-Dee-Doo Revue, when Dad declared that my husband and I were "no longer part of this family unit." He summarily kicked us out of the hotel at Fort Wilderness village. It's hard to find a car to rent at Disney World on Christmas Day.

Later that week, we got home to a letter from Dad. "Please take your husband's last name," he wrote. "You don't deserve to carry mine." For months my dreams were vivid and violent. I dreamed I would pay him back every penny he ever spent raising me. Maybe that would unmake him my father. Then I dreamed I would take a hammer to his kneecaps.

I thought of him almost daily, my anger mixed with a yearning for reconciliation. Years passed with no contact until my first child was born. As a new parent, I could not imagine feeling anger and disappointment sharp enough, or pervasive enough, to ever cast off my child. How could Dad have done so, felt so? How wounded my father must be, how damaged his soul from his own father's stern disapproval that never abated before he died. While nursing my son one day, I decided I would reach out to him.

On Father's Day I mailed him a bag of pistachios. I sent no note. He sent me back the empty shells. No note. But I smiled, and I imagine he did too.

> **—Name withheld at the request of the author, who reports that the process of forgiveness is ongoing and can be a tough nut to crack.**

THE GROCERIES

Who would have thought that something as ordinary as a bag of groceries could have such a profound effect?

I am a recovering alcoholic who has been clean and sober for about twenty years, thanks in large part to my dad. He got me my first and only adult job working with him on the railroad, but I made several bad decisions along the way, including making time for my friends at the bar after work, but not for my family at home. Divorce soon followed, and my dad and I grew further apart. I finally bottomed out at thirty-five and completed a second stay at a rehab center.

Sitting on the couch one afternoon and feeling bad about how I had screwed up my relationship with my dad, I decided to get happy at the nearest bar. As I was putting on my coat, there was a knock on the door. Standing there, holding a bag of groceries, was my dad, who said, "I thought you might need a few things and a hug." Boy, did I ever. "It doesn't matter what has happened," he told me. "You will always be my son."

I took the groceries from his arm and pulled up a couple of lawn chairs on the porch. For the first time in our lives we shared a moment without any small talk about the weather, or sports, or my job. Dad was a veteran of the Normandy invasion, but we had never discussed it. That day, for some reason, I told him how proud I was of him, and how I wished I could find the courage to fight my demons, like the courage he had shown by going overseas to fight for freedom. He then told me how much courage it took for me to have gone through the program a second time and said I should share my message of sobriety. I was floored. All the AA meetings came down to having the courage to stay sober and the opportunity to help others. That was a turning point; I have been sober since that day, and I was able to get my life together.

Time went by, and in February 2001, when I was traveling, I received a call telling me to get home right away because Dad wasn't going to make it through the night. I got to the hospital in time, and the nurse said that if there was anything I needed to tell my father, this was the time to do it. I leaned over and kissed him on the forehead and thanked him for that special moment on the porch. A few minutes later, a peaceful calm filled the room as he passed away. Even though he couldn't speak, his heart remembered what his mind may have forgotten.

—RICK BETHUNE, Saginaw, MI,
engineer, son of William Bethune,
railroad yardmaster (1923–2002)

The
Provider

**"If you don't work,
you don't eat."**
—Pat Anzalone,
father of
Scarlet Lento

As a child, I didn't exactly volunteer that my dad was a sanitation man. It wasn't something I was eager to advertise, so I found other ways to say it. And so did Dad. He would tell people he worked for the streets department, and I would bump him up a notch and say that my dad worked for the city.

Ironically, I began to feel better about Dad's job when I started going to a prestigious private high school. Many of my classmates' fathers were doctors, lawyers, and business executives, and when I met a few of them, I had a greater appreciation for my own father. It's not that I disliked these other dads, but in contrast to some of them, mine was down-to-earth, direct, and plainspoken. With Big Russ, there aren't many subtleties. You always know where you stand.

At the same time, I used to wonder what life would be like if I **had** been the son of a professional man. I might have gone to a fancier college, and certain doors could have opened for me, but none of those possibilities seem important to me now. What does seem important, especially as I read the many letters that came in, is how hard many fathers worked and how much they sacrificed for their children.

I realized only in retrospect that every father in this chapter is, or was, a blue-collar man. This wasn't intentional on my part, but I'm sure it reflects my pride and gratitude that Big Russ worked at two unglamorous jobs to support his family and send my sisters and me to Catholic schools. I saw that same fierce pride and deep gratitude in some of these letters. One man reported that his father worked three jobs: He drove a bus during the day, a taxi at night, and a beer truck on weekends. "I was one of ten children," he wrote, "and I thought this was normal."

Most of the sons and daughters in this chapter grew up in modest circumstances, but they don't seem to remember any significant deprivation. They also grew up in a different era, when kids didn't feel any pressure to own hundred-dollar sneakers, personal computers, cell phones, or iPods. What their dads gave them was a feeling of comfort and security, even when money was tight. As one woman put it, "He brought home the bacon, and every slice counted." In a less materialistic society, we were more than satisfied.

In most families I knew, Dad brought home the paycheck and Mom spent much of it at the grocery store. But when it came to food, Big Russ liked to eliminate the middleman. Dad rarely arrived home empty-handed. His only consideration was freshness; he rarely passed by a farm stand or a bakery without pulling over. He even taught me how to read the codes on a bottle of beer, so I could identify the freshest product at a time when that information was hidden from the public. He brought home the bacon, all right, along with the strawberries, the peaches, the cherries, the corn, and a loaf or two of freshly baked bread. I was blessed with a dad who literally put food on the table.

THE PLUMBER

This is one of my favorites, probably because it's a story of blue-collar revenge.

My dad was a plumber for the public works department in our town of Stratford, Connecticut, so from time to time he came into my school. Can you imagine sitting in class and seeing your dad peek through the door of your classroom and wave at you? In junior high?

One girl in our class always made fun of me because my dad was a plumber and hers was a lawyer, and she would say things like, "Ew, that's gross!" I must admit I was sometimes embarrassed by what my dad did, especially in my early teens, when the only thing I really cared about was what the other girls thought.

This girl lived a few streets away from us, and one winter day—the day her older sister was getting married—the toilet in their main upstairs bathroom cracked and there was water everywhere. Her father the lawyer called every plumber in the Yellow Pages, but nobody would come out because we were having a major snowstorm. His daughter told him that my father was a plumber, and he called, and my dad went right over—and took me with him. (Maybe he was hoping that the lawyer's daughter would be nicer to me.) My father fixed the toilet, helped them clean up everything, and didn't take a dime for his trouble. But as we were leaving, he told the girl, "If I ever need a lawyer, I'll be happy to call your dad."

As we walked to our car, he said to me, "Do you believe he didn't know where the main shutoff valve was? What a dumb ass!"

From that point on, her dad was known in school as Attorney Dumb Ass.

When my husband and I bought our house, the first thing my dad showed him was the main shutoff valve.

I have always been proud to say that I am a plumber's daughter.

—CATHY SLOSAR, Huntington, CT,
travel agent, daughter of
Edward W. Holden Sr., plumber
(1925–1997)

THE BULL

He was a well-dressed example of the American dream.

Growing up, my grandfather could not feed his family, so my dad and his brothers spent four years in a New Jersey orphanage until their parents could afford to care for them again. Dad was proud of having graduated from the eighth grade, but that didn't help him get a job. As a teenager during the Depression he was another mouth to feed, so he became one of the hoboes who rode the rails and moved around quickly to avoid being caught and sentenced to a prison chain gang.

In 1934 he married my mother and settled down to a factory job in New York's garment district, where he spent the next forty-four years pressing dresses in a sweatshop. He hated his job but was proud to have his children visit the factory once a year. He wanted us to see hard labor so we would strive to become white-collar workers like the "real" Americans, as opposed to himself, the son of Italian immigrants. Dad believed that the marvel of America was that anyone could rise above their birth status. The stock market meant he could own a part of America. He subscribed to **The Wall Street Journal** and read it cover to cover. He called it his college education.

Here's the amazing part: Each morning he put on old clothes to stoke the fire and walk the dog. Then he wore a suit to take the train from the Bronx to Manhattan, reading the **Journal** while holding a strap in a swaying subway car. When he arrived at the dress factory, he changed into his work clothes. At noon he put on his suit again and walked over to Merrill Lynch to watch the big board. He started by buying one stock, but he sold it before it got too high; he had read that there was a place in the market for both bulls and bears, but not for pigs. "Leave something for the next guy," he would say. He then bought another stock, and another.

After lunch he returned to the factory and changed back into his work clothes. At quitting time, it was back into the suit and tie for the train home, bringing the paper with him to finish reading after dinner. At home he dressed for the seventh time, this time in his comfortable clothes. He did this every working day for forty-four years.

When he died in 1987, this man who had

earned ten to twenty-five cents for every dress he pressed had amassed $140,000 in cash through his various stock purchases. He had also been able to buy a house and car and finance his retirement. With her small condo, the interest on Dad's cash, and her social security, Mom is able to live very comfortably. And all of Dad's children and grandchildren attended college and have fulfilled his dream of becoming "real" Americans.

—**Dorothy Cox, Bradenton, FL, retired facility manager, daughter of Jack Gioachino Federico, presser (1910–1987)**

THE BICYCLE

It wasn't perfect, but his son understood that it was assembled with love.

My first bicycle was a Christmas present when I was seven. This was in 1943, right in the middle of the war years, and there wasn't a new bike to be found anywhere. All available metal, including scrap iron, was being used to support the war effort.

At the time, I just had to have a bike. I can remember pleading with my dad for one (Santa having been exposed as a fraud during the previous year)—any kind, as long as it had two wheels. He was very patient with me and explained that it just wouldn't be possible that year. Deep down I understood, but a little begging never hurt, so I persisted.

Christmas Eve finally arrived and I looked everywhere; there wasn't a bike in the house. But as I came downstairs the next morning, my eyes almost popped out of my head. There, right next to the Christmas tree, stood the biggest, most beautiful red and silver bicycle I had ever seen. I don't think my feet even touched the bottom stairs as I dashed to inspect that miraculous sight.

The bicycle had big widespread handlebars, a bright red frame, silver fenders, and a large leather saddle supported by two coiled springs. But the most impressive feature was that it had just two wheels. What a wonderful sight to behold!

There was a light dusting of snow Christmas morning, and I had to wait another whole day before I could take that bike for a spin. Soon I was happily riding all around the neighborhood, oblivious to everything but the wind in my face.

Several days later, I began to notice a couple of imperfections on my marvelous machine—an almost invisible dent on a fender, a little smudge in the paint—just enough to make me realize that the bike wasn't new. I waited a few days, trying to get the courage to ask my dad where and how he got it. When I finally asked, he told me how he and a friend had scoured swap shops, junkyards, and other friends' basements looking for bicycle parts. After a month of searching, they had three unworkable bikes from which they assembled my red and silver beauty. Dad was somewhat apologetic as he told the story, but there was no need to apologize for giving me the best Christmas present I ever had.

—FRANK A. ZEDIK, Vestal, NY,
retired, son of Frank J. Zedik,
state trooper (1907–1988)

THE LABORER

**During tough times he kept the fire
going. He kept the family going, too.**

My parents married at eighteen and had ten
children. In 1930, when I was six, my father
got involved in the labor union movement and
lost his job because of it. The Great Depression had arrived and the job market began to
dry up, so he went from door to door in
Waukegan, Illinois, asking whether people
had painting, paperhanging, or other odd
jobs for him. He swallowed his pride and
went to township offices to plead for help.
Every other day or so, he brought home a
bushel basket of coal in a little red wagon,
coal he found along the railroad tracks where
it fell from coal cars and trains. He soled our
shoes on a last in the basement, shoes that had
already been passed on from one child to the
next. He put layers of cardboard in his own
shoes to cover the holes so he could walk to
the local factories and wait outside all morning for the labor bosses to choose day laborers.
Sometimes he was chosen, more often he
wasn't.

He demonstrated his love by the small things he did each day. He was always the last one to bed and the first one up. That meant banking the coal stoves so they wouldn't go out during the night, and fanning them back to life in the morning. By the time we got up, we could flip from front exposure to rear exposure in front of the hot stove, keeping at least half of our body warm while we dressed. He always had water heated on the stove for washing faces and hands, and a pan of cocoa, made with one part cocoa, two parts canned milk, seven parts water, and a bit of sugar. He made toast on some kind of wire contraption on top of the coal stove. Whenever possible, he insisted that my mother stay in bed with whoever was the current baby, and he brought her a tray with cocoa and toast.

Thanks to Daddy, we never knew we were dirt poor until we were grown. He protected us from it all. He saw that we were fed, even though our food was largely beans, peas, and whatever he could raise in a small garden. We were housed, even though we had to move frequently to places with cheaper and cheaper rent. When he talked to us about those moves, he made them seem like exciting adventures. Most of all, we always knew we were loved and would be cared for.

—**Patricia Youngman, Waukegan, IL,**
retired office manager,
daughter of Edward T. May,
handyman (1900–1983)

THE MINER

He loved his family too much to say good-bye.

Daddy never said good-bye. I first noticed it the year I turned five, when he used to drive Mother, my brother John, and me from our shanty at the coal mine into Madisonville, the heart of the west Kentucky coalfields. "Be good babies," he would say to John and me before he left us to wait with Mother in the car when he went inside to night school, where he was earning a certificate in mining safety that would entitle him to a raise.

He had gone to work in the mine when he was fourteen, three years after his father died and left the family destitute. When the foreman learned that Daddy was underage, he sent him home; Daddy waited two years and went back to the mine. He had been there ever since. He didn't complain about his lot, but he was determined that his children would have more education than he did. He worked days and studied nights to get a better job, so he could save enough money to move us away from the mine, where there was no high school, into town, where there was.

He never said good-bye when he left for work. "Be a good baby," he would say, throwing me a wave. It wasn't what I wanted to hear. Other kids had dads who said good-bye. Why wouldn't mine?

Finally, Mother explained. Daddy never said good-bye because he was afraid of a fatal mining accident. He thought if he never said good-bye, there'd never be one.

It was an irrational response to a rational fear, but I didn't know it then. It would be years before I understood the hazards of Daddy's occupation, the risks he willingly assumed to support our family, and the fear that he and Mother looked squarely in the eye and stared down every morning when he stepped onto the "cage"—an open platform—and descended into the belly of the earth.

One day a coal-blackened man appeared at

our front door at midday, a sight guaranteed to strike fear in the hearts of every miner's family. The roof, the overhead structure above the seam of coal in a mine's working area, had caved in on Daddy, the man said. An ambulance had already driven him to the hospital.

The hospital stay was short; the recovery was not. Daddy lay in bed at home for weeks, his pelvis fractured. The only cure was keeping his weight off the bone until it knit back together.

The summer heat was insufferable. Unrelenting humidity hung thickly in the air, plastering our damp clothes to our moist skin. It was an extra burden for an active man forced to lie in bed in a shanty with no air-conditioning, but Daddy's only complaint was that he couldn't go to the mine.

As far as I know, he never considered not going back. Coal mining was all he knew; as risky as it was, it was how he fed his family. And it was how, ever so gradually, he accumulated the meager savings that allowed him, when John was twelve and I was eleven, to move our family into Madisonville. Living only a block from the high school, John and I earned diplomas. Daddy valued them for the education they represented; we valued them for the sacrifice he made that allowed us to attain them.

Decades later, while installing playground equipment at a church, Daddy succumbed to a fatal heart attack—no symptoms, no warning, and no fatal mining accident. It was an appropriate passing. The man who never said good-bye never had to.

—**CAROLE HARRIS BARTON, Burke, VA,**
retired government analyst,
daughter of Samuel Sterling Harris,
coal miner (1911–1983)

THE MILKMAN

You've heard of taking your daughter to work? This was an earlier variation known as putting your daughter to work.

My dad was the father of eleven children. Instead of going to college after the war, he stayed home to manage the family dairy business started by his grandfather in 1908.

When people ask me when I started working, I say, "As soon as I could carry milk."

From the time I can remember, I hopped for him, which means that as he stopped the truck at each house, he would clap, and I jumped off the truck with the milk carrier, a steel case that held eight quarts, ran my fastest into the house, unloaded the milk, exchanged pleasantries with the customer, made change, and ran out of the driveway, where he would drive to the next house. This fast-paced method allowed us to finish our home deliveries by 1 P.M., when I could then collect my pay—either a quart of chocolate milk or lunch at Henry's Hamburgers, a McDonald's precursor. It was a huge treat to have lunch out, so despite the hard work it was worth it.

After lunch, we would start the commercial deliveries to the local stores. While Dad did the heavy lifting, I would straighten the truck, load the empty cases, and try to look busy so as to not get any more assignments. At the end of the day, I was required to count the receipts, put the paper money in order and face up, and give him an accounting of the day. My milk route job started when I was seven and continued through college, when my dad sold the dairy in 1985 upon his retirement.

Dad was not a chauvinist: I had to work as

hard as my brothers, and from the start I was lugging heavy milk cases. I worked the milk route on Saturdays, holidays, and summers.

Dad worked Monday through Saturday. He couldn't call in sick, as his customers relied on him. The mothers on his route stayed home with their families and didn't have a second car to go out shopping during the day.

He only missed one day of work, during western New York's infamous blizzard of 1977, when the snow prevented him from getting the truck out. The next day we were back on the route, making up for lost time. Non-customers kept stopping us and asking for milk, and Dad sold everything that day without adding a penny to the price.

My dad was an early riser, and he wouldn't let us sleep in. Especially in the winter, he would yell, "You lazy kids! All the other kids on the street are out shoveling. Get out here!" It wasn't true. The other kids were watching cartoons. But we ran out, ice choppers in hand, and cleared the driveway to the pavement. He was right there with us, shoveling for hours, and it wasn't uncommon for six of us to be clearing the snow all at once.

Most of us are runners and have completed numerous marathons. I attribute our love for running to the fact that Dad never allowed us to slacken. He would say, "Chop-chop!" and clap his hands, and we would run everywhere. It sounds funny now, but I can still hear him say it.

—PATRICIA FARRELL, Buffalo, NY, financial adviser, daughter of Neil R. Farrell, milkman (1922–2005)

THE DRY CLEANER

Miami would have been easier, but Iowa seemed like a better choice for his kids.

My dad was born in a very small town outside of Bogotá, Colombia. He was the second of seven kids and the oldest son. His family was very poor, and his dad died when he was only twelve. He immediately quit school and went to work in Bogotá so he could support his family.

He found employment at a laundry and dry-cleaning plant. The owner of the laundry took an interest in my dad and was impressed with his determination, his maturity, and his dedication to his family. As he grew up there, the owner asked about his goals and aspirations. My dad told him that his dream was to take his family to the United States so that his kids—which at that point consisted of a baby boy (me)—could have the best educational opportunities.

The owner was so impressed with Dad's determination that he sent him to a dry-cleaning institute in Washington, D.C. My dad had only an eighth-grade education and spoke very little English when he arrived, and he started off getting D's and F's on his exams. Staying up till all hours of the night, he scoured through a borrowed English-Spanish dictionary to be able to understand his study materials. He ended the year with B's and graduated from the institute.

During his time in Washington, he asked around: "Where is the best place to raise a family in the United States?" Everyone told him to move to the Midwest, which happened to coincide with his goal to move somewhere that did not have a large Hispanic population. This would force us to fit in. A beautiful family in the town of Oelwein, Iowa, took a chance on my dad and hired him for their large laundry and dry-cleaning plant.

His next challenge was persuading Mom to give up everything that was comfortable to her and move to the middle of the United States. She didn't speak a word of English, and they were moving to a town where almost nobody spoke a word of Spanish. Fortunately, he was able to convince her.

We moved to Iowa in July 1968, with very little money. But the little town of Oelwein was perfect, and the people could not have been nicer. When we arrived, a couple of our neighbors took Mom to the grocery store and the post office to show her how things worked in the United States. We thrived there, and my parents had two more children. When I turned eighteen, my parents and I became naturalized U.S. citizens. I was fortunate enough to attend and graduate from the U.S. Air Force Academy. The air force sent me to law school, and I am currently a lieutenant colonel, stationed at the Pentagon.

Maybe my father knew where my future would be. Once, when I was a little boy, we went to the airport, where he pointed to the men unloading luggage and directing the planes. "These people are making an honest living and they have nothing to be ashamed

of," he told me. Then he pointed to the pilots.
"But if you can do better, why not?"

—JUAN-CARLOS GUERRERO,
Haymarket, VA, attorney,
son of Carlos Guerrero, dry-cleaning
superintendent (1937)

Missing Dads

"I could justify almost anything with, 'If my father were alive, he would approve.'"

—JANET ROGOZINSKI, daughter of James G. Richardson

Growing up, I didn't know about families who were missing a father, because there weren't any in our neighborhood. I became more aware of this problem in high school, when a friend lost his dad to a heart attack. (Almost nobody was divorced back then, or so it seemed, especially among Catholics.) It wasn't until I worked for Senator Moynihan that I started to become aware of the effect of missing fathers on the larger society.

Back in 1965, while working in the Johnson administration, Moynihan had written a report called "The Negro Family: The Case for National Action." In it, the young social scientist described the ongoing breakup of black families, in large part due to absent fathers. The nation was shocked to learn that 24 percent of black children were born into single-parent families. Four decades later, that number has reached 69 percent, and figures for the Hispanic and white communities have shown similar upward trends. In 2005, the percentage of all American children born into single-parent families was 35 percent—more than one child in three. This is very bad news: The correlation between single-parent families (at the time of a child's birth) and poverty is painfully high. Many children born in these circumstances do manage to achieve extraordinary success, but that is far from the norm.

I talked about this not long ago with Charles Barkley, one of the NBA's best-known and most outspoken players. Barkley, who grew up without a father, pointed out that the lack of financial support is only part of the problem, and that a boy needs a dad for another, more basic reason: to learn how to become a man. As he put it, "You don't know how to be a man unless somebody teaches you."

To be sure, most of the letters in this chapter address other aspects of absence: fathers who leave, die, or disappear after the birth of their child. Reading these letters, I flashed back to February 1997, when John Kennedy Jr. appeared on **Meet the Press** to talk about his magazine, **George.** At the end of the show, in what we call the "Meet the Press Minute," we ran a film clip from December 2, 1951, when the future President Kennedy was a young

Massachusetts congressman. At the time, JFK was thirty-four; when John Kennedy Jr. appeared on **Meet the Press,** he was just two years older than his father had been then. As he watched the footage of his father, our guest was mesmerized; it seemed to me he was studying his father's face. He was three when the president died, and he told me (off the air) that his actual memories of his dad were so intertwined with all the film clips he had seen that it was impossible to tell them apart. He asked to see the clip a second time, and we left him alone to view it. Even if your father is the most famous man in the country, a missing dad is a missing dad, and if he was your dad, a part of you is missing as well.

The stories in this section make clear, in a more personal way than the Moynihan report possibly could, that a family without a father puts children at a real disadvantage. The impressive thing about these sons and daughters lies in how some of them came to terms with their reality while others, against the odds, were able to overcome this obstacle by finding an alternative father—or even, in one case, a virtual dad—to give them the comfort and security that they otherwise would have missed.

THE DREAM DAD

A beautiful example of making the most out of very little.

My father died when I was less than two years old. I have no memory of him, and my widowed mother, in her pain, moved on, remarried, and never mentioned him again. I grew up without an image or likeness to understand who I came from. But I also grew strong and responsible, hearing in my head endless advice that I was sure my father would have given me, had he lived. In a way I had the best of imaginary fathers, because I could justify almost anything with, "If my father were alive, he would approve." With age and wisdom, I learned that the fantasy had served me well.

After I turned forty, my mother gave me a photo of my father in uniform during World War II, so strong and handsome. With three children of my own, I suddenly turned into a daughter for a few weeks, staring at the picture. Each night I would kiss him good night, touch his cheek on the photo, look into his eyes, and wonder what he was thinking. I somehow bonded with the father I never had.

—JANET ROGOZINSKI, Potomac, MD, economist, daughter of James G. Richardson, civil engineer (1921–1955)

UNCLE LOU

Sometimes the truth is ugly, and there's no point in pretending otherwise.

The estrangement between my father and me began eight days after I was born, when my twenty-six-year-old mother suddenly passed away. Soon enough I'd be branded with a litany of not-so-flattering adjectives. "Bastard" had already been established. "Motherless" was added to the list.

My father was burdened with other commitments, like raising his own family and dealing with the pangs of lost love. I've never envied the man. Dad was Jewish. Mom was Irish-Catholic.

Grandmom Mickles and Aunt Dinny raised me. They were good women, and I didn't lack love and care.

My birth certificate identified me as Louis Christine Jr., done purposely by Mom, since in those days children born out of wedlock had "Illegitimate" stamped on their birth certificates. I was told that my father owned his own cab under the banner of United Cab of Philadelphia, number 425. Starting around age six, I paid attention to decals on cabs, but I never saw a trace of cab 425.

When I was seven a visit was arranged. "Go out and play," my grandmother said. "We'll call you when he comes."

A big man stared down at me. He mentioned how my little boy's hands had turned a ruddy red from the cold. A nervous-looking woman in a black overcoat sat close by. My father handed me some money and told me to buy myself a pair of gloves, but the rest of the visit melded into grown-up talk. Dad and the lady soon faded into the winter's day.

I often scanned the white pages. My father's West Philadelphia address and phone number were listed under the name Rose Christine. I would touch the print and ponder the what-ifs. My grandmother and my aunt had different surnames. I was the only Christine I knew of.

Another birthday came, and I received a card addressed to Master Louis Christine. Along with a five-dollar bill were two signatures, **Uncle Lou and Aunt Rose.** Grandmom was livid. She insisted I dial a sequence of numbers, my first phone call ever, to ask why the card was signed **Uncle Lou.** A man's voice answered, and I eked out Grandmom's request. First a silence, then a disconnect. As far as I know, my father never again tried to contact me.

I was nineteen, on leave from the army with orders for Vietnam. On a whim I drove to West Philadelphia. I found myself standing in front of a bank of doorbells: CHRISTINE, APT. 204. I rang. The door buzzed open and I moved down a hallway. A man appeared in a doorway, in his sixties, cigar in mouth, wearing glasses. He said nothing and offered only a cigar-chomping scowl.

I gathered my voice. "Are you Lou Christine?"

He answered in salty Edward G. Robinsonese, "Who wants to know?"

"Me, Lou Christine," I said evenly.

There wasn't so much as a blink. "C'mon

in," he mumbled. "Wanna drink or something?"

I probably told him I was leaving for Vietnam. He spoke fondly about my mother, but
mostly about himself. He showed no interest
in who I was. He ended the one-sided conversation by telling me he had to run to the bank
before it closed.

Again he fished into his pocket. He plucked
out a twenty and said, "Go buy yourself a meal.
Good luck over there. Better watch yourself."

I said I wasn't there for a handout.

"Whaddaya, crazy? Go ahead. Don't be a
putz."

The man was self-centered, boring, and
ugly. He was also bald, the way I've become. A
sagging belly screened any sign of a belt
buckle. On my way back to the car I tortured
myself for not asking questions, but he never
offered an opening.

More years passed. I was married and raising
a boy whom I eventually adopted. I met my
wife and her son when he was ten months old,
and didn't want that boy to live a fatherless existence. One day, with three-year-old Robby
tagging along, I decided to show the old bug-
ger that I had the right stuff to raise a son.

His wife answered and recognized me immediately. There were some awkward moments, but Rose whipped up refreshments and treated us both with dignity. The old man said little, other than asking if I was making a living. He seemed more interested in the newspaper, and we soon left.

More years passed. I hadn't paid my parking fines. In traffic court the bailiff barked, "Louis Christine." I walked toward him, but he called my name again.

"That's me," I said.

Another voice piped in. "That's me!"

There stood my father. The packed courtroom let out a chuckle. So did the judge. I turned toward my father and said, "Hey! What are you doing here?"

Lou Christine Sr. volleyed, "What are **you** doing here?" as if we were part of some Abbott and Costello routine.

There was another round of laughs. The judge smiled and grabbed his gavel. "Dismissed!"

Outside, I asked, "How ya doing?"

"Fair to middling," he mumbled.

"Wanna get a cup of coffee or something?"

"Nah, busy. . . . Gotta go."

More years passed. Aunt Dinny had cancer. On Thursdays I'd chauffeur her to a medical center. While waiting, I'd mope outside near the entrance of a busy pharmacy. To my left sat a taxi in a NO PARKING zone. It was United cab 425.

He was just inside the pharmacy, using the pay phone. For me, the once-joyful anticipation of such a find had long faded. My stare toward the man was as hard as Pennsylvania coal, but my innards were topsy-turvy. He looked at me as if I were wallpaper.

He hung up, let out a sigh, and was about to walk in front of me. Street sounds muted. Action shifted to slow motion. Drumbeats pounded inside my brain. I could taste the smelly cigar and sensed an empty soul. The thumping sounds subsided as he moved on and ducked into the cab. Like that, he was gone.

A clerk came from behind a counter and peered down at the cigar ashes on the carpet. "Did you see that jerk? Always asks for change, never so much as a thank-you, and drops his ashes all over the floor."

I shrugged. "Takes all kinds, I guess."

I never saw him again. He died penniless of

a heart attack at seventy-three, wallowing in the crummy bed of a twenty-three-year-old woman, a heroin addict.

I've wondered if his fatherly sins would trickle down to me. In many ways they have, but perhaps because of other fundamentals, I've had guidance and opportunity to reach a higher plane; at least I hope I have. For too long I thought I had missed out on something, yet with time and circumstance I have come to realize that, all in all, it was dear old Dad who missed out on me.

—LOU CHRISTINE JR., San Miguel de Allende, Guanajuato, Mexico, writer, son of Lou Christine Sr., cabdriver (1905–1978)

THREE YEARS

She knew him only briefly, but their time together really counted.

My father was thirty-six when he died of leukemia in 1953. For three years he had fought this disease, after being given six months to live. I was only three at the time, and I was told that my father vowed to live long enough so that I, his only child, would remember him. And I do. I remember his laugh, his love of music, and, most of all, how he loved my mother and me.

But the thing I cherish most of all is that, as sick as he was, I don't remember those three years as "sick years." Even after he was in the hospital more than out, there were trips to the zoo and to the lovely parks in Memphis, where we would feed the pigeons and just seize the joy of the moment.

My mother never remarried. She said she had had the best, so she never went looking for a replacement.

My daddy passed on to me his love of people and his sense of humor. Not a day goes by that I don't say, "Thank you, Daddy, for living long enough for me to remember you."

—LaVale Mills, Red Bay, AL,
newspaper publisher,
daughter of Veto Lee Kennedy,
farmer (1917–1953)

THE PILOT

He never really knew his father, but almost half a century after his death he was able to learn a great deal about the man.

My dad died suddenly in 1952, when I was only two. During World War II, he had been a copilot on a B-24 Liberator. On August 3, 1944, on his twentieth mission, he was shot down over Ehrwald, Austria. He spent the rest of the war in three different POW camps, where he suffered from starvation, forced marches in freezing temperatures, and God knows what else. Seven years later he succumbed to a massive heart attack, a direct result of his imprisonment in Germany during the war.

For years, first as a young boy and then through adulthood, I wondered what kind of man my dad had been. My mom rarely spoke of him, and I'm sure the pain and sorrow of losing her husband was unbearable. Although I would often hear that he was a kind, loving, and generous person, I wanted to know more. One day, in 2001, that desire became a reality.

Through the Internet, I was contacted by Gerd Leitner, an Austrian who, as a child, had witnessed the air battle in which my father's plane was shot down along with seven other American bombers and five German planes. The event stayed with Leitner and became his obsession. He researched and compiled records of all the men, both American and German, who were involved on that horrible day, and he invited them, or their surviving family members, to meet together in Austria on August 3, 2001, the fifty-seventh anniversary of the air battle. His purpose was to commemorate and honor these individuals.

I attended the event, together with my older son. We spent hours with the navigator of my dad's plane, sitting on his every word as he told of their training together, their missions, and their experiences as fellow POWs. We climbed high into the Austrian Alps to visit the crash site of my dad's plane. Words can't describe the emotions I experienced on that mountain, especially when I was able to retrieve—and bring home—the copilot's seat where my dad had sat throughout his missions. And I met a woman, who, as a young girl, had actually seen my father captured by the Germans and had proof that it was really him. When my father went off to war, he had taken with him, as a memento from home, his first child's baby shoe. The woman who witnessed his capture remembered that one of the American airmen had shown a tiny shoe to his captors to let them know he was a father.

Especially after the events of 2001, I am aware of the incredible sacrifices that my dad and his fellow soldiers made to ensure our freedoms. As we lose over a thousand World War II veterans a day, I hope that future generations will never forget what these men and women did.

Dad, I wish I could have gotten to know you and love you more, but after meeting friends of yours and being in places where you used to be, I feel I know you better. I have never felt closer to you.

—Jim Kurtz, Danvers, MA,
millwork manager,
son of Robert R. Kurtz, credit manager
(1919–1952)

LARRY'S DAD

Material things are not the key to being a father. And sometimes, neither is sharing the same name.

Our family seemed to have it all. My father was the son of a well-known explorer, and my mother was a debutante who had attended all the right schools. We, their five children, went to the best schools, wore beautiful clothes, traveled abroad, and seemed to live charmed lives. But behind that façade was psychological abuse and rampant alcoholism.

In high school, I fell in love with a wonderful young man. His loving family adopted me, and I learned that you don't need great wealth to lead a rich life.

Although he had five children, Larry's father never missed a game, a school event, or anything else his children were doing. When it was time to rake the leaves in the fall, everyone raked the leaves. When it was time for dinner, everyone helped serve and clean up. Each child had chores to do, and the older ones taught the younger ones. They all learned to love golf, which they played at the local public course. Each child went to college, and they were allowed to pick the school and their major. They also had to help with the tuition.

They spent their vacations together on a lake in New Hampshire, with bunk beds in every room so friends could visit. Each child's success was celebrated. I learned about love because Larry's father loved these children with every fiber of his being.

Two of these children, Larry and his sister Tracey, had cystic fibrosis. Although they spent countless hours in doctors' offices and hospitals, Larry's father treated them with the same high expectations, love, and care as his other three children. Larry and Tracey were both athletes—which was unheard of at the time for CF patients—and they participated in every family activity. Although their life expectancy was said to be twenty-one, they both lived well into their forties, leading full and productive lives. I am convinced this was because their father treated them like the other children in the family.

I didn't marry Larry, but years later, after I was married with children, I sought out his father to thank him for showing me what a real family was all about. His children knew every day without fail that he loved them, supported them, and would be there for him. To me, he is the quintessential father, and each Father's Day I visit his grave, where he is laid to rest with Larry on one side and Tracey on the other. As he wished, he continues to be surrounded by his family.

—TRACY A. TAMER, Latham, NY, administrator, "daughter" of Richard Roche, insurance executive (1924–2002)

THE STRANGER

Sometimes a father just leaves, and you never learn the whole story.

My father was a soldier during World War II and returned home an injured and broken man. He met my mother at a Red Cross hospital in California where she was a social worker. As far as I know they never lived together, and I'm not sure they were legally married. After he was released from the hospital, he lived alone in a hotel in downtown Los Angeles. I don't know how he earned a living. He died in 1952.

I was born in March 1946. In April, he

made a visit to my grandparents' house in Los Angeles. In the photograph I have, he is standing on the front lawn, dressed in a suit and tie, holding me rather awkwardly in his arms. I like the look on his face. He seems a little uncomfortable, but I like to think he was proud. I have always wondered why he came that day—and never again.

Did someone tell him to stay away? And if so, why did he listen?

He never was able to give me a home or family but he did give me my name, Cynthia Jeanne. This has always been the one gift from him that I could treasure. There really is nothing else.

Owing to his poor health and, I suspect, alcohol abuse, and probably other reasons too, I don't think my father ever saw me after that day in April. There were no letters of advice for me at college, no birthday cards or correspondence of any sort. No phone calls, no sound of his voice, and no footsteps. No laughter or smell of his cologne to remember him by. The day I was married, I walked myself down the aisle. I always wonder what gifts and traits and stories he could have added to my world. I know my life would have been richer if he had been a part of it. I chose to believe he was an honest, caring man who did the best he could, given his circumstances. But I wish I could have done something to help him.

—**Cynthia Jeanne Wall,
Marlborough, NH, office manager,
daughter of Oscar Frank Chambliss,
occupation unknown (1909–1952)**

THE STEPFATHER

They got off on the wrong foot, and their relationship was bad for many years. Then she became a parent.

My first childhood memories of my stepfather were filled with resentment because he wasn't my "real" daddy, with whom I remembered laughter, presents, and happy times. My stepfather was always saying no, criticizing my behavior or the way I dressed, and dragging me to church, so I assumed he didn't like me.

One memory is especially vivid. When I was ten, he promised me "two bits a row" to weed the green onions in our garden. They were two very long rows, but I was willing to squat and pull weeds for over two hours in the hot Texas sun to earn four dollars. When I finished, I was bitterly disappointed when he plunked fifty cents in my dirty, sweaty little hand.

"You said two dollars a row!" I protested.

"No, I said two **bits** a row. That's fifty cents." And he laughed, which infuriated me. Certain that he had cheated me, I whined to him and to my mom, but he wouldn't budge. It would have been easy for him to fork over another $3.50, but he said, "A deal is a deal."

During my teenage years, things got worse. My swimsuit was too small, my skirts were too short, and I couldn't stay out past ten or play certain kinds of music. I was forbidden to see movies that all my friends were going to, like **The Graduate** and **The Exorcist.** Missing church on Sunday was unthinkable, despite my frequent Sunday morning illnesses. The peace-sign posters in my room had to be taken down—unpatriotic **and** unchristian—along with the psychedelic posters. All the while, I was daydreaming of how wonderful my life would be if only my "real father" was there.

I was probably thirty before I started seeing my stepfather in a different light. By then I had a son of my own, and I had begun to wonder why my "real" father had never visited me while I was growing up. But my stepfather was always there. By the time I was forty, I had raised my son and was aware of the challenges of molding and shaping a child to have integrity and strong moral values. By this time, I could see that my stepfather's determination to keep me safe and instill good values in me was not because he didn't love me but because he did. At last, my stepfather and I reached common ground, and I finally appreciated his wisdom. We spent many years gardening together before he passed away a few years ago. Not a day goes by that I don't miss him and think about the lessons he taught me. And I can't look at a green onion without thinking about him—and smiling.

—KATHY STEED, Texarkana, AR,
administrative assistant,
stepdaughter of Fred "Tommy" Thomason,
U.S. Navy, retired (1919–1994)

Memories

**"Hugs are free.
Someday, when I'm
not around, you're
going to want one."**
—SALVATORE N.
GERACI,
father of Joe Geraci

Because we didn't have much money when I was a boy, my sisters and I used to give our parents Christmas presents that we had made ourselves. When I was seven, I took an empty tomato sauce can, peeled off the label, and covered it with tinfoil. Then I took a roll of sticky tape with a holiday pattern and taped down my father's initials: TJR. (The T was easy, the J was a backward L, and the top curve of the R was a little V-shaped, but he got the idea.) I bought three items to put inside the can: a ballpoint pen, a number-two pencil (was there any other kind?), and a real treat for Dad—a cigar. Yes, in those days a kid could buy cigars.

Years later, on a visit home from college, I went into the house to look for Dad. I thought he was in his bedroom, and although I didn't find him there, I did see, on his dresser, my Christmas gift from years earlier. The pen and the pencil were still there—along with the school pictures of his four children, in a neat stack, which he had saved over the years. I took a deep breath. My dad, whom I didn't think of as sentimental at all, had saved my modest gift all these years—and, what's more, he was still using it to hold other precious memories. I didn't linger; I had other things on my mind, like borrowing his car. But one day, when Luke came home from school with a little holder he had made for my desk, that sweet memory of Dad came rushing back.

THE HAIRCUT

**A kitchen is no place for a haircut—
except when it's your dad.**

The year he reached eighty-five, I turned fifty. His was an active, robust life, working outside, building things, laying bricks, shaping archways and columns for the eyes of another generation; beer and whiskey in the saloon with the guys on the way home—I knew the routine. I'd spent a summer, laboring, pushing a cement-crusted concrete buggy down splintering plywood runways in the steel skeleton of a hospital addition we'd worked on. From what I'd overheard, I knew he was proud to have me there with him. I was his kid, home from college.

"Hair's getting shaggy. Can I cut it?" He had given in to letting his mind wander and to gazing off. He turned the wineglass slowly. He wasn't wearing his hearing aid; he never did. The controls were too delicate for rough fingertips that had worked with concrete blocks and masonry for fifty years.

"Can I give you a haircut?" I offer again, louder.

As though startled by my presence, although we'd been together in his kitchen for the last hour, he turns to me.

"No. . . . What for? I go no place."

"Maybe you'll get a date."

He smiles; a front tooth is discolored, another chipped. He'd been as handsome as a movie star. Pictures of him and my mother (a victim of leukemia twenty years earlier) aboard the **Andrea Doria** are fresh in my mind. A factory seamstress and a bricklayer, it had taken them years of saving to afford this vacation back to Italy, the first since their Ellis Island processing.

I find the barbering smock in the sink cabinet. Comb and scissors are in the bathroom. A razor, soap cup, and brush with bristles soft and splayed are on the windowsill. There are more times now when my ideas are rejected, but I proceed, knowing that his resistance will abate. He doesn't want to relinquish control, not yet; never, I hope.

His eyes are closed; his chest rises and falls in the long slow rhythm of breathing; he appears to be asleep. Sunlight glints into the room from between the slats of the dusty venetian blind. Clippings lie on the floor and on the cotton throw. Mama would have had a fit over a haircut in the kitchen. She would have pulled me by the ear and walked me through the back door. "It's not a barbershop. It's a place to eat."

I run the narrow-tapered end of the comb through his eyebrows and clip off white thatches that stand up like picture wire. I carefully clip the hair that grows out of his nostrils, the nose chiseled on a profile that could be minted. I snip the short, softer hair on the edges of his ears. I bend an ear forward to get at a follicle. He grimaces, but I know there is no pain. He loves me to cut his hair. At ease, content, he settles back in the warmth of soft, gentle stroking.

I swirl the old brush in the cup and lather under his chin. He'd shaved earlier, before my visit. I finish what he'd missed on his neck. I wipe the soap away from his ears. I fill my palm with witch hazel from an ancient bottle and pat it gently on his face. I rub his neck; my fingers move up under his ears. I remember him when he was so young and strong. I remember him carrying me on his shoulders out into the surf at Long Branch and building my clubhouse in our backyard, where I displayed on its walls pictures of my favorite Yankees and Bob Feller. I remember wine-making every October in our musty cellar.

He lives alone now in the house where I'd grown up with my sisters and my mother and grandmother. He had a hand on every inch, inside and out. He planted the fig trees and nurtured them like children, wrapping them carefully to survive the winters. He built the grape trellis and fieldstone fireplace next to our patio. His face is in my hands. He looks at me through eyes hollow and clouded.

"Gotta go. See you next week."

"Huh. . . . What?" His forehead furrows.

"Gotta go. Got work. See you next Tuesday."

He grabs my hand. His grip is still strong. "Come early," he says. He doesn't see the tears as I turn for the door.

"I love you, Raim," I hear him say. It had taken him fifty years to say it, but it wasn't necessary. He had told me many times, in many ways.

—RAYMOND PASSACANTANDO,
Whippany, NJ, retired insurance agent,
son of Alfonso Passacantando,
mason/bricklayer (1900–1987)

THE VISITOR

He couldn't afford the bus, but he also couldn't afford to arrive empty-handed.

I loved my dad very much, but I really didn't know him. My two brothers and I were put in an orphanage at a very young age because he couldn't take care of us. We were allowed visitors once a month, and I remember sitting on the front steps, my eyes glued on that long driveway, hoping that my dad would show up. And he did. He lived in Louisville, six miles away, and he walked six miles to visit us because he couldn't afford the bus fare. But he always brought some kind of little toy.

He was buried in Shepherdsville, Kentucky. I am seventy-three now, but someday I hope to go there and see his grave. To this day I can't talk about my dad without getting choked up.

—CHARLES "MIKE" LASLEY, Union, OH,
retired factory worker,
son of John Lasley, railroad worker
(1880–1944)

THE LUNCH BOX

How do you put a value on your dad's most basic possessions?

It's just a lunch box, and it's not even mine yet. Dad turned eighty last year, and all signs point to his outliving me. But of all the things my dad owns—and he has some very nice stuff—that lunch box goes to me. Let my brother and sisters battle for the rest. I know what I want, and I know why.

It's not a rare antique, although my father owns a house full of antiques. It's a plain black worker's lunch box, dented and scratched, its latches held closed with a steel pin. When the handle broke off in the sixties, he made a new one out of copper tubing.

When I was little, my dad worked at a trucking company. He worked all night while Mom and I slept, and he took that lunch box with him seven days a week, except Christmas. Mom made his lunch and I packed it: two sandwiches, a hard-boiled egg, some fruit or precious leftovers. Whatever it was, I added cookies and a napkin. "If God wanted us to use a napkin, he wouldn't have invented long sleeves!" he'd laugh. Off he went, the sound of his old truck carrying him away.

In the morning there was often a treat waiting for me in that lunch box, but more often than not there was just the napkin that God didn't want him to use.

Inside that lunch box are scents of food I haven't smelled since Mom passed away fifteen years ago. In that box he carried fuel for an honest-to-God working machine. He earned a living with that fuel and gave us a home that was safe and secure. Every night I got to participate by loading it up and handing it off. With a dad who worked so hard, this was one of the few things we did together. For me it always seemed enough.

I've held many jobs in my life, several careers in fact, and through it all I still match myself to the image in my heart of a real working man. I've raised five sons of my own, and sometimes I have seen that look of respect in their eyes as I head out to do for them what he did for me.

The lunch box sits in the cupboard in Dad's kitchen, where he put it after his last day of work in 1985. It's still there, but I have resisted the temptation to take it out and open it. There will be a better time to do that. I'll pop the latches, lift the lid, and catch the scent of one last lunch. And I know I'll find the napkin that God didn't want him to use.

—CRAIG JAMES, Medina, OH,
taxi company owner,
son of Frank James, garageman (1925)

THE MAIL

He knew his father was special to him, but he hadn't realized that everyone in town felt the same way.

As a young boy, I sometimes traveled the country roads with my dad. He was a rural mail carrier in southwestern Michigan, and on Saturdays he would often ask me to go on the route with him. I loved it. Driving through the countryside was always an adventure: There were animals to see, people to visit, and freshly baked chocolate-chip cookies if you knew where to stop, and Dad did. We made more stops than usual when I was on the route because I always got carsick, but stopping for me never seemed to bother Dad.

In the spring, Dad delivered boxes full of baby chicks. Their continuous peeping could drive you crazy, but Dad loved it. When the peeping became too loud to bear, you could quiet them down by trilling your tongue and making the sounds of a hawk. When I was a boy it was fun to stick your finger through one of the holes in the side of the cardboard boxes and let the baby birds peck on your finger. Such bravery!

On Dad's final day of work on a beautiful summer day, it took him well into the evening to complete his rounds because at least one member from each family was waiting at their mailbox to thank him for his friendship and his years of service. "Two hundred and nineteen mailboxes on my route," he used to say, "and a story at every one." One lady had no mailbox, so Dad took the mail in to her every day because she was nearly blind. Once inside, he read her mail and helped her pay her bills. And every Thursday he read her the local newspaper.

Mailboxes were sometimes used for things other than mail. One note left in a mailbox read, "Nat, take these eggs to Marian; she's baking a cake and doesn't have any eggs, and don't stop to talk to Archie!" Mailboxes might be buried in the snow, or broken, or lying on the ground, but the mail was always delivered. On cold days Dad might find one of his customers waiting for him by the mailbox with a cup of hot chocolate. A young girl wrote letters but had no stamps, so she left a few buttons on the envelope in the mailbox; Dad paid for the stamps. One busy merchant used to leave large amounts of cash in his mailbox in a paper bag for Dad to take to the bank. On one occasion the amount came to $32,000. It's hard to believe, but it's true.

A dozen years ago, when I traveled back to my hometown on the sad occasion of Dad's death, the mailboxes I noticed along the way reminded me of some of his stories. I thought I knew them all, but that wasn't quite the case.

As I drove through Marcellus, I noticed two aluminum lamp poles, one on each side of the street, reflecting the light of the late-afternoon summer sun. When my dad was around, those poles supported wooden boxes that were roughly four feet off the ground. One box was painted green, and the other was red, and each had a slot at the top with white lettering: SANTA CLAUS, NORTH POLE. For years children had dropped letters to Santa through those slots.

I made a left turn at the corner and drove past the post office and across the railroad tracks to our house. Mom and I were sitting at the kitchen table when I heard footsteps on the front porch. There, at the door, stood Frank Townsend, who had been Dad's postmaster and great friend for many years. So of course we all sat down at the table and began to tell stories.

At one point Frank looked at me across the table with tears in his eyes. "What are we going to do about the letters this Christmas?" he asked.

"The letters?"

"I guess you never knew."

"Knew what?"

"Remember, when you were a kid and you would put your letters to Santa in those green and red boxes on Main Street? It was your dad who answered all those letters that the kids wrote every year."

I just sat there with tears in my eyes. It wasn't hard for me to imagine Dad sitting at the old oak table in our basement reading those letters and answering each one. I have since spoken with several of the people who had received Christmas letters during their childhood, and they told me how amazed they were that Santa had known so much about their homes and their families.

For me, just knowing that story about my father was the gift of a lifetime.

—JOHN MOOY, Interlochen, MI,
writer, son of Nat Mooy,
mailman (1905–1985)

THE TYPEWRITER

Can you imagine this father's fear for his family when the men in hats showed up?

Our family came to Portland, Oregon, in 1938, refugees from Hitler. One Sunday afternoon in 1943, when I was seven or eight, I was playing on the living room floor when we heard a loud knock on the door of our apartment. My mother opened it and shrank in fright at the sight of two large men in hats. "FBI," they announced, showing their badges. "May we come in?"

"Yes, yes," she said in confusion, shouting for my father.

The grown-ups sat down at the dining room table. Did we have a shortwave radio? the agents asked. No. Did we have a telegraph key? No. Did we have anything **like** a telegraph? No, my father said, his neck red with anxiety. We had the stand-up radio in the living room. Oh, he added, and a little portable Smith-Corona typewriter. He took it out of its black leatherette case and opened it.

Do you use it on this table?

Yes.

Ah, one agent said to the other. That must be it.

They explained. A neighbor, suspicious of my father's German accent, had heard all this clicking and tapping. Ignorant of what Jewish refugees had gone through, she concluded that we must be spies sending messages to the Nazis.

We're sorry to have alarmed you, the agents said. Maybe in the future you could put the typewriter on a phone book to muffle the sound, they said, retrieving their hats on the way out the door.

That was more than sixty years ago, yet the moment lives on.

—JACK ROSENTHAL, New York, NY,
foundation president,
son of Manfred Rosenthal,
judicial administrator (1907–1975)

THE TAG

You may not see it, but he feels it.

A few weeks after Dad was buried, I was going through his personal effects. I opened his wallet, where I found a dollar and a couple of pictures of his four granddaughters. I pulled out his driver's license, and out fell a tag like the ones you get on your Christmas gifts. I looked at it closely, and on the back, written in my mother's hand, was a note that said, **He tried to write his name, and he wanted me to ask you, "When are you coming home, Daddy?"**

This man, whom I used to think I could never satisfy, had carried around, for forty-seven years, a note from his wife and two-year-old son from Christmas 1944. I learned from this that a father's love is an enduring thing. Sometimes it's hard for children to see, and sometimes it's hard for fathers to show, but that love is always there.

—H. John Brandel, Wingate, NC,
communications contractor,
son of John J. Brandel, hospital
superintendent (1916–1991)

THE NOTES

Some fathers are silent. Some fathers talk. And every now and then you find one who puts his feelings in writing, a few words at a time.

My father, a pharmacist, owned a drugstore in downtown Detroit, where my mom served as his accountant. My brother and I liked to say that our father was a druggie and our mother was a bookie, but our parents didn't think that was funny.

He loved to write notes to his children, especially when we returned from school to an empty house. Here are three of my favorites:

My loving children,
    I am going to work and Mom will be coming home soon. Be comfortable and content and you will be a comfort to your mother and to me. Do not burden your conscience so it will not burden you.
Your loving Dad

Laurie & David,
    Mom is driving me to ~~drink~~ work.
Dad

And my favorite, truly his final farewell:

> Dear children,
>
> I have gone to work to earn some money, your mother has gone to Sears to spend some. Entertain and look after each other so that you may inherit the earth. Look after your mother and treat her with respect so that your days will be long and happy, blessed with the fruits of gratification, bringing contentment and serenity with the knowledge that the sun will rise again and again.
>
> Dad

—LAURIE RUSKIN, Newton, MA, attorney, daughter of Harold Ruskin, pharmacist (1914–1998)

THE SALUTE

He died as he lived—with dignity.

Daddy was an old-fashioned barber, the leather-and-porcelain-chair, hot-lather-machine, straight-razor-sharpened-on-a-leather-strop kind of barber, not the frou-frou beauty-salon-stylist fancy-smelling-products kind. His barbershop was my after-school refuge, with its hot lather, those steaming hot towels, the smell of blue tonic in which black plastic combs stood, and piles of hair on the floor.

He was always the room mother when I was in elementary school—an oddity in the 1960s, the only man amid a bevy of women—icing black and orange cupcakes for Halloween and greasing the pig for Field Day. As a young girl, I would hold hands with him and gently step onto his perfectly shined hard black leather wing tip shoes, one socked foot on each shoe, to twirl a bit. He was particular about those shoes. They slept with wooden posts inside them, so dancing on them was an honor as well as a pleasure.

Many afternoons Daddy treated me to a fake shave, lathering my face and imparting words of wisdom as he held me captive under a hot towel wrapped efficiently like a white cinnamon roll. Once when my next-door neighbor upset me by disagreeing about something important to my ten-year-old mind, he bundled me in a hot towel and said, "Honey, there's an old Yiddish saying: 'If we all pulled

in one direction, the world would keel over.' "
I never did learn how this Southern Baptist
came to be quoting a Yiddish proverb.

My life was irretrievably altered when Daddy
died, too young at fifty-three to be going anywhere, much less that far away without at least
a snack. Fifty-three seemed old to my teenage
self, but it seems shockingly young now, as I
grow nearer to it myself.

A young man named Leon worked in the
barbershop, second chair from the door.
When Daddy sold the shop because of his
heart, Leon left to be a policeman. Five years
later, as the processional with the last bits of
Daddy and over two hundred cars made their
way to the cemetery, there on a traffic island,
alone and at attention in full dress uniform,
one white-gloved hand over his eye at a full
salute, the other holding his hat over his heart,
was Leon—a moving tribute to a small-town
barber who was so much more than that.

—PATRICIA DIGH, Asheville, NC,
diversity consultant,
daughter of Melvin Lonnie Digh,
barber (1927–1980)

The Protector

"It'll be your ass if anything happens to her."

—John Paul Fox,
father of
Ruthann Fox-Hines

During the summer between elementary school and high school, I noticed a little peach fuzz on my face. The time had come for me to shave, I decided, so I went down to our basement bathroom, covered my face with Dad's shaving cream, picked up Dad's safety razor, and started in. Never having shaved before, I pressed the razor as hard as I could. A moment later, I looked in the mirror and saw a character out of a horror movie.

Frightened, I grabbed a wad of toilet paper and pressed it against my face as I tried in vain to stop the bleeding.

Just then, Dad noticed the basement light on. "Who's there?" he called.

"Me."

"What are you doing?"

"Nothing."

"What do you mean, **nothing?**" He came downstairs and said, "What's wrong?"

"I'm so sorry!" I told him. "I'll buy you a new razor."

"Don't worry," he said. "We can take care of this."

He took out his styptic pencil. "Hold my arm," he said. "This will sting a little." When the bleeding finally stopped, he put gauze on my wound and covered it with a bandage.

"Are you gong to tell Mom?" I asked. For some reason that seemed to matter.

"Well, Mom's going to see this."

"Are you going to tell her what I did?"

"We'll think of something," he said reassuringly, adding, "Mom won't understand shaving."

Mom was out, and when she came home, Dad spoke to her privately. When she saw me, all she said was, "Dad said you scraped yourself." I was relieved. Now that I'm a parent, I realize that Dad probably told her the truth, that he probably said, "Timmy cut himself shaving, but he doesn't want you to know, so let's say I told you that he scraped himself."

Kids often try to align with one parent against the other, and sometimes a parent's role is to play along with that desire—to advocate and be the protector for their son or daughter. Most kids probably have no idea how much their parents think about them, worry about them, and talk about them with each other, and it's probably best that way. Becoming a parent is the greatest moment in your life, but it's the last worry-free day you'll ever have.

Oh, yes—a few years ago, when Luke started showing some peach fuzz of his own, I made sure he knew how to shave. He probably knew already, but I was determined that my son would not repeat his father's painful mistake.

THE NET

She didn't know it at the time, and wouldn't want to have known, but Dad was there for her, even at sea.

My mother died when I was twelve, and my father, a former ship's master who inspected ships in Hampton Roads, Virginia, was left to raise a budding teenage daughter on his own. Although he was experienced in many areas, he had almost none when it came to bringing up a daughter. Sometimes he was overprotective, and we often butted heads, but there was always love and respect between us. I suspect he did a great deal of praying.

When I finished college at nineteen—the local one, because he wasn't letting me go off anywhere—I started teaching in a parochial school. By the summer, a friend was able to arrange passage for me to Europe on an Italian coal freighter sailing out of Norfolk. Poppa didn't stop me, and I had thirteen wonderful days as queen of the sea on the **Gabiano,** living out my fantasy of following in my father's footsteps.

I was the only passenger and the only woman. The bursar gave up his room for me (I never knew where he bunked). I dined with the chief engineer and the captain, and the three officers and the radiomen entertained me—all very properly. I was told that the captain was unusually nice, and that the men were getting over their superstitions about having a woman on board. It was a great adventure.

About ten years later, after I was married with a school-age son, my father told me the real story. When I announced my plans for a sea adventure, he immediately called the owners of the shipping company that owned the **Gabiano** and said, explaining that his daughter would be on board, "It'll be your ass if anything happens to her."

He didn't stop me from having an adventure because I was a girl. He let me have it, and the confidence that came with it. Without my knowledge, he provided a safety net. He had run off to sea at sixteen and was a ship's master by twenty-three. I think he realized that if I had been his son, there would have been no stopping me, so instead of preventing me from going, he did what he could quietly to extend his protective arms without getting in the way. Although he is gone now, I still talk to him and ask him to keep that invisible safety net in place.

—RUTHANN FOX-HINES, Columbia, SC,
counseling psychologist,
daughter of John Paul Fox,
steamboat inspector (1900–1981)

THE CARETAKER

He put his girls first—even when they were all grown up and his life was ending.

My sister and I are both single and in our fifties, and Dad had always helped us with everything. Then, suddenly, the roles were reversed. I took my father to the doctor, where he learned he had a tumor in his esophagus. I drove him home and said, "What do you want to do about this?"

"Whatever you want me to do," he said.

"Let's see what the specialist says," I told him.

Ten days later I took him to an oncologist, who told us that Dad had only three weeks to live. "In all my years of treating cancer patients," the doctor said, "I have never seen so much cancer in one body."

Dad extended his hand to the doctor and said, "I've had a good life, Doc, and I thank you for being honest." Somehow I held myself together, knowing that if I broke down and cried it would only make Dad feel worse.

We got in the car and headed home. When I came to a stop sign, he said, "Back up here and pull into this garage. I want to make sure they're working on your sister's car, so she won't have to go without one for long." He had just been told that he had three weeks to live, but he never stopped taking care of us.

He didn't have any pain. Three weeks to the day, he went to sleep one night and didn't wake up. But he was our father to the very end.

—PEG EVERHART, Huntingdon, PA,
mail inspector, daughter of
Donald P. Everhart, quality control
(1927–2004)

THE DANCER

Her dad took care of her when she developed polio. And he continued to protect her when she and the family had to face a worse fate.

My dad had a Hawaiian mother and a German father, a combination that gave him the quiet strength, sweetness of countenance, and willpower to deal with everything he encountered. His humor and passion for living endured till the day he died.

When I contracted polio as a small child, he knew he had to raise me as normally as possible. So although I had steel braces on my legs, he taught me how to dance. He would gently place my feet on top of his shoes and strap my braces around his legs with a belt. The Victrola played a slow Viennese waltz as he spun me around the room. I was enthralled as he laughed at our newfound discovery of pure joy. I danced with my father all my life as he took me through many wonderful dance steps.

As Americans living in the Philippines during World War II, we were imprisoned by the Japanese Imperial Army for over three years.

We suffered great deprivation of food and freedom, and experienced malnutrition and all its complications

During the last fourteen months, our meals consisted of one ladle of watery rice each, three times a day. We would hear my mother scold my dad when he dipped his bamboo spoon into his portion and gave each of us three kids an extra spoonful, even though he was hungry himself. She was frightened that he would not hold up under his heavy daily workload: digging ditches, hauling heavy equipment, cutting firewood, and other jobs. But he continued to share his meager rations with us. My father was a hero to me because I saw for myself what he did.

—SASCHA JEAN JANSEN, Vacaville, CA, retired, daughter of Walter Weinzheimer, sugar planter, farmer (1904–1985)

THE STREETS

You don't have to be on great terms with your son in order to give him permission to save his own life.

At sixteen, I was an out-of-control, selfish, irresponsible kid. We lived in a housing project in Rockaway Beach, New York, and my dad was a sanitation man and a part-time waiter in an Italian restaurant. Although he used up all his favors and connections to keep me in high school, I finally quit, which broke his heart. I worked all day and drank all night. I was in a tailspin, headed for serious trouble.

I decided to join the army and figured that I just had to wait for my seventeenth birthday. But a seventeen-year-old needed both parents' permission, and Mom refused to sign the papers. (This was during the Vietnam war.) A few days later I went to see Dad at his sanitation station, and for maybe the first time in our lives we connected. I played on his military experience—he had served in the South Pacific during World War II—and begged him to talk to Mom. Less then a month later I was Private Walter A. Arcario at Fort Jackson, South Carolina. Dad even taught me how to sight and shoot a rifle—over the phone. I was sent overseas, but to Europe rather than Asia.

While I was in the army, some of the guys I knew back home wound up on drugs, in jail, or dead. Meanwhile, I was becoming a better man. There are no snooze alarms in the army. You have to be where you're supposed to be, and you had better be early. My goal was to get out with an honorary discharge, and I did.

Some thirty years later, shortly before Dad passed away, I asked him why he had supported my decision to join the army at such a young age. I had two sons of my own by now, and I needed to know. He pulled me close to him, looked me right in the eye, and said, "I would never have been able to live with myself if I lost you to the streets." Thank you, Dad.

—WALTER A. ARCARIO,
Rockaway Beach, NY, safety consultant,
son of Joseph B. Arcario Sr., sanitation man
(1914–1994)

THE BIG MAN

A daughter's pride in her dad comes in all sizes.

I was about four, and we were at Bradley Beach, New Jersey, when I somehow lost my way between the water and my family. I wandered the beach, terrified. All I could see were legs. I couldn't find my way back. I cried. Finally I heard someone call "Andrea!" It was my father, and I ran to him. He picked me up and carried me back to our blanket. I was safe.

He always made me feel safe. Physically, he was a big, strong man. When I was a kid, he seemed huge to me. Not fat, just big. He stood just over six feet tall, but his strength came from the broad chest and big stomach.

My father loved to eat. He could not be left alone in a bakery or a delicatessen, or he would "buy out the place," as my mother would say when he came home on Sunday mornings with bags filled with whitefish, onion rolls, and apple turnovers.

I loved his bigness. I loved that he could pick up my bicycle with one hand and carry it out of a sudden rainstorm. I loved how he could carry my overpacked suitcases and load them effortlessly into the car for the drive to college. When he developed diabetes in his late fifties, the doctor made him lose the gut. He lost thirty pounds and became slim. I knew he was healthier, but I hated how he looked and I never got used to it.

—ANDREA MEISELES, New York, NY, educator, daughter of Monroe Meiseles, hardware salesman (1927–1994)

THE STRONG MAN

Get ready for a real Kodak moment—a fridge with feet.

My dad was only five foot ten, but everyone called him Big Al. He spent his adult life doing manual labor—mostly construction work—but despite the long hours, Dad always had time for others. If I close my eyes, I can still hear the garage door going up on a Saturday morning and the two-wheeled dolly being loaded into his pickup. He was always helping somebody move something. If you needed a favor or wanted something moved, you called

Big Al. He was always there with a strong back and a big smile.

When I was five, we were moving to a new house about a block away, and the strap to the dolly was broken. Dad looked at our mammoth fridge, and he looked down the street at the new house. Out came the inside shelves, and then Dad got inside, lifted the fridge on his back, and started walking. All you could see was this refrigerator at a forty-five-degree angle moving down the street with two legs sticking out. Mom was yelling, "Al, you're going to have a heart attack!" We heard that a lot over the years. But Dad was laughing and moving down the street, one step at a time. Our neighbors began to gather, and I remember standing with some kids on the sidewalk, swelling with pride. My dad was the strongest man in the world, and everyone knew it.

—**STEVE ROYER, Elkhorn, NE,**
software executive,
son of Al Royer, cement finisher
(1931–2000)

Tolerance

"He had been spiritually wounded by the racism of his day but never became embittered by it. He still believed that people were basically good."

—JOYCE TURNER HEATHCOCK, daughter of Kenneth L. Turner

Some years ago, when General Colin Powell was chairman of the Joint Chiefs of Staff, I drove over to the Pentagon to meet with him. During my visit, when I asked him to direct me to the men's room, he said, "Actually, we have twice as many of those as we need in this building."

"Why is that, General?"

He explained that when the Pentagon was built in the early 1940s, the state of Virginia still practiced segregation, so the builders put in separate bathrooms for whites and "coloreds."

Maybe I shouldn't have found that shocking, but his comment stopped me in my tracks. We like to think of racial segregation as something that happened long ago, but in certain places, and in a lot of memories, there are still some vivid reminders of that unhappy era.

I grew up in an all-white neighborhood in a northern city, with parents and teachers who talked often about racial tolerance. The Sisters of Mercy at the schools I attended used to tell us that man was created in the image of God, and that the spirit of God could be found in every human being. Of course not everybody practiced what the nuns preached, and the n-word was sometimes heard on the streets of our neighborhood. But not in our house. Once, when my older sister told a story that included the word **Polack,** my sister Kathy, who was probably around seven, reprimanded her. "B.A., you're not supposed to say that. You're supposed to say **colored person.**" Kathy was a little confused, but she had the right idea.

My father, who worked with men from a wide variety of backgrounds, used to talk to us about not making assumptions on the basis of somebody's skin color, and judging from the letters I received, so did many other fathers, for on no other subject did I read so many similar stories. When Dad was a foreman in the streets department and heard that Jimmy, one of the workers on the garbage trucks, was making ugly comments about blacks, he teamed him up with a light-skinned African American. A couple of weeks later, Jimmy told Dad that his new partner was a good, hard-working Italian kid.

"He's not Italian," Dad said. "He's colored. And I hope you learned something." I know that story because Dad came home and told it at our dinner table.

Although our society is far from perfect, in recent years we have made real progress in racial equality and religious tolerance. Legislation and judicial rulings are the instruments of change, but a fair and just society really depends on individual acts of respect. Our hearts are formed when we are young. The letters in this chapter demonstrate the unique importance of a father's good example.

THE REAL STORY

Actions really do speak louder than words, as his daughter was delighted to learn.

From everything I could see, my father was a racist. He spoke in derogatory terms about the black men who worked for him. "A lazy crop of humans," he said, "spending their pay on booze and leaving their women to care for all those children." Conditioned by my Girl Scout education, I was acutely sensitive to the plight of black people. I would rail at my father's generalizations and his inhumane assumptions, but I got nowhere. I was ashamed of him and took great pains to make sure that none of my friends ever engaged him in a conversation about race.

Once, when I tried to talk with him, Dad said, "When you've seen as much of the world as I have, you'll realize that people are not as good as your Pollyannaish spirit believes."

When I countered that there were plenty of no-count whites, Dad shrugged and said, "Someday, maybe you'll understand." I continued to regard my father, who was normally so compassionate and understanding about other people's problems, as a bigot, and he indulged me as a bleeding heart.

At the age of sixty-five, Dad died unexpectedly of a heart attack. As was the custom in Baltimore, there was a viewing of the deceased before the funeral, where the family was expected to escort the mourners to have "one last look." I hated the process, but as a dutiful daughter I escorted various friends and relatives—all of them white, with the exception of our black laundry lady, who told me that Dad had always thanked her for the way she ironed his shirts. "Like a queen, he made me feel," she sobbed. Then, as the last of the visitors hurried in, I was sought out by a gigantic black man. "You must be the daughter," he said, as he clasped my hand. "I'd be most appreciative if you'd walk up with me to view your daddy for one last time." His strong grip left me no choice.

"I'm not sure I know you, Mr.—?"

"No, ma'am," he whispered. "I'm the dispatcher at the company. Just call me Joe. You know, if it wasn't for your daddy there, I'd be sweeping up the dispatch room and washing down walls and mopping floors. But your daddy saw something in me and helped me work my way up to be a dispatcher. He was always there for me—when my wife got sick, when the children acted up, even the time I was arrested for getting a little drunk. He was the one person I could count on. Yessir, Mr. Frank was the only white man who really understood what it was like to be colored."

I squeezed his big black hand with unbridled compassion. Joe had given me a remarkable gift. He taught me to have faith, no matter what the outward signs might indicate.

—CELESTE ULRICH, Eugene, OR,
retired professor, daughter of
Frank G. Ulrich, transportation
supervisor (1903–1968)

TAN SKIN

He was no longer around, but she gave him the benefit of the doubt because he had earned it.

My father would have loved my children. He was born in 1889, and some of his eight older siblings were born while the family still lived in a sod hut on their Dakota Territory homestead. His world was very different from mine, but my father would have loved my children.

This may not seem like such a remarkable statement; most people love their grandchildren. But some do not, especially when their beloved daughter marries a man of a different race and has children with tan skin and curly little Afros. My teenage son looks like he just escaped from a rap video, with baggy pants and a big crystal in his ear, but my father would have gotten a huge kick out of him. He would have loved that my son inherited his gift for math, he would have loved his sense of humor, and he would have loved him because he is mine. He would have loved my daughter because she is such a great listener and would sit attentively as he told stories of graduating from high school at fourteen because he read through all the books in his one-room school-house. He would have told her about manag-ing a classic old hotel in Rapid City, South Dakota, and having President Roosevelt visit, and the man who carved Mount Rushmore living there. He would have been impressed that she could put anything together, even without the directions.

I won't deny that a racially mixed marriage might have been a little difficult for him to get used to. After all, I grew up in the fifties in a town where a mixed marriage was one between a Lutheran and a Catholic. And even back then, people asked, "But what about the chil-dren?"

But he would have gotten used to the idea, and he would have loved my children.

My father was a man of some dignity, but he wasn't careful with his language. He never hesitated to call someone an SOB if he was one or to identify BS when he heard it. But the only way I ever heard him describe a black man was as a "colored gentleman," and this was long before I ever met anyone who wasn't white. What he cared about was a person's character.

His health began to fail when I was in high school. And some days, when I came home from school, I would find him sitting in his big wingback chair facing the bookshelves. On the shelves were pictures of each of his children. He once told me that he went from picture to picture much of the day, stopping at each of the five and saying a prayer, because that was now his only way of taking care of us. He thought we were the best. My father died a few years after that, but if he had known my children, he would have thought they were the best, too.

—SUSAN DeMERSSEMAN, Berkeley, CA,
psychologist, daughter of
Bert DeMersseman, businessman
(1889–1965)

FATHER OF THE NEIGHBORHOOD

He had every right to be angry, but he still completed his mission.

My father was born in 1917. When he was eighteen, he built and flew an airplane. I remember him, late in life, describing how he converted an old Chevrolet car engine into an airplane engine. He wasn't able to get the plane too far up in the air, but it did fly, and some people who witnessed this feat still talk about it.

He was drafted into the army during World War II and was deployed in the Solomon Islands and the Philippines, where he saw active duty in an all-black company. Only late in life did he tell me that he had continually applied for flight training until a white officer told him that his applications were pointless, because when it was known that he was black, his paperwork was thrown in the trash. Although the news broke his heart, he always said it was an honor and his duty to fight for his country.

After the war, my father was known as the father of the neighborhood in our section of Indianapolis. Anyone in need could call on him and he would find a way to help. He fixed cars, radios, televisions, furnaces, air conditioners, and did plumbing and electrical work and charged nothing. He bought groceries for people he knew were in need, and we were not a wealthy family. He loved unconditionally and always strove to see the good in people. He was a magnificent, courageous, generous, caring, loving man who had been spiritually wounded by the racism of his day but never became embittered by it. He still believed that people were basically good.

—JOYCE TURNER HEATHCOCK,
Indianapolis, IN, computer operator,
daughter of Kenneth L. Turner,
supervisor (1917–1998)

THE OFFERING

She broke his heart, but his love for her was strong enough to overcome his bias.

I grew up in South Buffalo, where my claim to nonfame was that I was a Protestant. (I was born on St. Patrick's Day, which gave me some standing.) I envied all my friends dressed in their First Communion outfits and tagged along to do the seven churches on Holy Thursday. But all through my childhood, my father kept warning me not to be taken in by the "hocus-pocus mumbo jumbo" of the Catholic Church.

He was my rock. He had never finished high school and worked most of his life at a coal plant. Our first and only house had cost him $2,500, and it remained the source of his greatest joy. The only place we ever went was to visit relatives, and we never, ever, ate in a restaurant. We shopped for clothes only when necessary, and played canasta and rummy at night while eating popcorn and listening to the radio.

When I was accepted at Mercy Hospital School of Nursing, my father had a fit because of those conniving Catholics. Finally, with the persuasion of Sister Mary Ellen, he allowed me to go. One night I was caught out after hours at a tavern, drinking beer by the pitcher. Sister Mary Ethel drove down there, walked in, and expelled us on the spot. I had to call my dad to come and pick me up. This was the lowest point of my life, and I was devastated because I knew I had hurt him deeply. But no words were ever spoken.

The next day he was gone all morning, and when he came home he told me to get in the car. He pulled up to the nurses' residence and proceeded to unload packages from Sears, Roebuck and Western Auto. I had no idea what was going on, but he marched me right into Sister Mary Ethel's office and asked her to take me back. He then pulled out a clock for the foyer wall, a new twenty-five-cup coffeemaker, and a huge box of chocolates. I was mortified, but Sister Mary Ethel accepted the peace offering and I was reinstated. That clock hung there for years, and it always brought back the memory of my father saying, "Honey, there had better never be a next time." And there wasn't.

After graduation I moved to Westchester County and worked in a hospital. I had been a Catholic for about a year, and after another year or so I decided to enter the convent. This meant really hurting my parents, and it was a struggle I endured for another year. Finally I took the coward's way out and wrote to them of my intentions. Two days later, my father showed up to try to talk some sense into me, as his worst fears had come true. The Catholics had stolen his daughter.

At the convent, he met with Mother Mary Mark and some of the other Franciscan sisters. When the meeting ended, he was laughing and joking with them. I almost fainted. My father, who thought nuns were the female rejects of society, had made peace with his worst fear. As we walked to the car, he said, "They're not a bad lot. They even let me smoke my cigar." We had a real heart-to-heart talk that night.

"Well," he declared, "you will never make me a grandfather, but to see you happy is an answer to my prayers." One of the girls I entered with was Eileen Paul, the daughter of Ralph Paul, the announcer on the **Ed Sullivan Show.** My dad thought this was really great, and the two of them became fast friends.

I could come home only once a year, but when I did, Dad had everyone he knew at the house. He was so proud! When we visited the World's Fair in New York, he loved the respect that people showed me, especially when it put us at the head of a long line. The good sisters loved my father, and when they visited Buffalo, he and my family would take them to see the sights.

My father died of cancer at sixty-two. I had come home to be with him, and all over his room were pictures and letters from the nuns and their students. He had a Lutheran funeral, surrounded by Sisters of Mercy, Franciscans, and two Catholic priests.

The people my father once perceived as his enemy had become his biggest allies, and it happened because he never let anything get in the way of his love for me.

Ten years after I entered the convent, I left,

married, raised three daughters, and never let anything get in the way of my love for them. My dad taught me well.

—**KAREN ANDRUSCHAT, Wyoming, NY, nurse, daughter of Fred Rabe, factory worker (1901–1964)**

THE INSPECTOR

One man's junk is another man's dignity.

I have many fond memories of my dad, and the final one was in January 1967, after he died suddenly at the age of fifty. Walking into church for the funeral, I noticed a row of impoverished men, dressed in what must have been their finest clothes, sitting in silent, sad attention. These were the hoboes who hung around the railroad station, where Dad worked as a car inspector, and they were there to honor the man who had supported them for so long.

For years he had been bringing home square glass ashtrays with chips and cracks in them that he had purchased from these men who had nothing. I guessed that they had probably been lifted from restaurants or hotels when nobody was looking. We also had a large and unnecessary collection of flyswatters that Dad had also been buying from these men who had nothing. He always had money for them, and he knew it was better to buy what they had to offer, whatever its origins, than to give them a handout. He believed that, like anyone else, these men deserved to be treated with dignity.

—**JAN POPE**, Emily, MN,
nurse, daughter of Ray Ludwig,
railroad inspector (1916–1967)

MR. STRAWBERRY

A dad follows his heart, and a stranger becomes a friend.

When I was ten and helping out at my dad's liquor store, a man walked in looking disheveled and confused. He told Dad he had no money, his car had broken down, and he was trying to get home. Without hesitation, my father gave the man twenty dollars and called him a cab.

"Dad," I said, "that guy was a bum. Why did you do that?"

He said he could see from the man's eyes that he was telling the truth and was in trouble.

The following Christmas Eve, flowers were delivered to our business, addressed to Joseph Kelly and his son, wishing us a merry Christmas and signed **Mr. Strawberry.** For the next forty years, the flowers came without fail. I finally asked Mr. Strawberry, who had become a regular customer, why he sent us flowers every year. He told me that on one of the worst days of his life, on one of the hottest days of the year, his car broke down and he, a black man, was then mugged by three white teenagers while he was trying to get help. His insulin was low, he was dazed and confused, nobody except Dad was willing to help him, and he would remember that as long as he lived.

—**Joseph Harrison Kelly,**
Bordentown, NJ, investment adviser,
son of Joseph Harold Kelly,
liquor store owner (1925–2003)

THE COINCIDENCE

**Her father stood up when it counted—
and she remembers.**

Although my father achieved professional success and financial comfort, he refused to leave the Bronx neighborhood that he and my mother were raised in. We lived in the same fifth-floor walk-up that my mother lived in as a child. When our neighbors decided to buy "a house on the Island," Dad refused to consider leaving the city he loved.

By 1963, white flight was beginning to transform our neighborhood, and before long the first African American child took a seat in my Catholic school classroom. Birthday parties were about the biggest social events a third-grader had to look forward to, and I was delighted to receive an invitation to her party. Then I learned that none of my friends was going. I remember being confused by that, because we all went to one another's parties. But if my friends weren't going to this one, I wasn't going to go either, especially when they seemed convinced that there was something wrong with the very **idea.**

I no longer remember the exact conversation, but Dad put his foot down and told me that, like it or not, I was going to that party. He took me to the five-and-dime and we bought a card and a gift. The day of the party, he took me by the hand and we walked the three or four blocks to the girl's apartment. My whining and complaining were useless, and it wasn't until many years later that I understood why he made me go. He knew why none of my friends was there, and he wanted no part of it. No child of his was going to contribute to the hurt that would surely be felt by a little girl sitting at an empty birthday table.

More than forty years later, this is pretty much the only childhood birthday party that I actually remember. I was treated like a very special guest by the girl's family, but mostly I remember it because of the laughter I caused when Dad came to pick me up, and I loudly pointed out that the girl's entire family was dark, just like she was. What a coincidence!

—MARGARET HACKETT, Highland, NY, legal clerk, daughter of James Hackett, fire commissioner (1912–1967)

BIG ADE

When a father doesn't brag, sometimes it takes until after he dies to know the full extent of his goodness.

My father was known as Big Ade, which was short for Adrian Francis Sauer Jr. He enlisted in the U.S. Army Air Corps right after Pearl Harbor, although he eventually washed out because of a fractured skull from childhood. He graduated from Infantry Officers' Training School at Fort Benning, where he was trained to help lead what would have been a suicidal invasion of Japan. The A-bombs were dropped on Hiroshima and Nagasaki just before he became a second lieutenant. These awful events probably saved his life and gave me mine.

Then he came home to start a family. He loved the army, but he didn't want to drag his family to army posts across the nation and around the world. Instead, he bought a luncheonette on the main street of Haddonfield, New Jersey. He called it Ade's Lunch, where he figured out that he was not in the food business as much as the entertainment business, and where people of all classes and colors ate in equality. In the late 1950s and early 1960s when the Yankees were in the World Series, Dad would rent a black-and-white TV to put on top of the phone booth, so his customers could join him in cheering for the pinstripes. His favorite player, and mine, was Yogi Berra.

Big Ade's second job was serving in the New Jersey National Guard one weekend every month and for two weeks each summer at Camp Drum in Watertown, New York. Dad loved the Guard, but Mom and my brothers resented it because of the time it took from us and the strains it put on the family business.

In the summer of 1967, his Guard unit was sent to Newark, where a riot had erupted and police were having trouble containing it. Dad went without having any idea how dangerous or how long his mission would be. When he returned many days later, he told us that his job was to drive through the fiery city in an open-top Jeep with his M-1 Garand and to ferry intelligence from one point to the next. He said there was enough gunfire to keep him on his toes, and that this was the only time in thirty-four years of military service that he had ever been in combat. That was all he said.

When Big Ade died a few years ago, we had both his memorial service and his wake in a local restaurant. There were old photos of him on display and artifacts from his sports career, Ade's Lunch, and the army. His favorite Glenn Miller music was playing in the background. The "celebration of life" was scheduled for 11 A.M., with drinks and lunch at noon.

Suddenly, at 10:45, thirty of Big Ade's National Guard comrades came into the room, most of them wearing caps with their unit's number on it. They greeted me as if I were their long-lost son and expressed their sympathies with tremendous warmth and a few tears. I immediately understood why my father treasured his Guard experience and had such love and respect for his buddies.

A clergyman friend of the family, who used to eat in Ade's Lunch when he was a boy, gave a great homily. I somehow made it through the eulogy I had written for my dad without breaking down.

Then, as I made my way around the large room to say thank you, one of Big Ade's old Guard buddies, Sergeant "Jeep" MacAdams, grabbed the sleeve of my suit. Jeep told me that it was my dad who encouraged him to go into the Guard after World War II, which saved him from driving a cab in Camden for the rest of his life. "There are so many stories I could tell you about your old man, Richie," Jeep rasped into my ear. "But let me tell you at least this one. . . .

"You know we were in Newark during the riots of 'sixty-seven. It was a combat situation, let me tell you. I want you to know what an excellent and brave soldier your old man was. He was a true leader.

"We were called to a building that the state police had their machine guns trained on. They said they needed backup because there were rioters in the building. They told us to help them take this position with tear gas, machine guns, grenades, whatever.

"Your dad challenged the state cops from the get-go. He asked them what made them think there were no innocent civilians inside the position. The state police were zealous, you see. They had already fired shots, and they wanted us to fire warning shots, but your dad asked them to please hold their fire. Then he volunteered to assess the situation. He stayed low and got to the big door of the building, which was locked, and he calmly announced, 'I'm with the New Jersey National Guard and I'm here to lead you to safety. Everything will be okay. Follow me.'

"Suddenly, about twenty-five black high school kids came out of the building behind him, shaking and crying. Your dad was comforting them with one hand and giving the 'hold your fire' sign with the other. He asked if they needed water or food. Rich, your dad treated those kids with such respect and kindness. If he hadn't gotten involved, I'm sure there would have been bloodshed, if not death."

This was what I learned for the first time at Big Ade's memorial service. Could I be more proud of him had he won the Congressional Medal of Honor? I don't think so.

—RICH SAUER, Ocean City, NJ,
nonprofit fund-raiser,
son of Adrian F. Sauer Jr.
(1922–2001)

Discipline

**"God loves you,
and I'm trying."**
—PETER DE MATTIA,
father of
Kevin De Mattia

In just about every family we knew when I was growing up, the mother was the nurturer and the father was the disciplinarian. That's how the roles were divided, and in many families it still is. As long as Mom and Dad were united and consistent in their approach, the system worked. And although Dad's disciplinary tactics were rarely appreciated by his kids at the time, I could have filled this whole book with grateful testimonies from sons and daughters who were at the receiving end years ago.

One man wrote about getting in trouble as a teenager for being part of a group of kids with rifles in their car. The police took them down to the station, and when this man's father came to pick him up, he expected a long lecture. Instead, to his shock and dismay, his father told the police, "Keep him."

He spent a day clearing brush on a road gang, he reports, and was never in trouble again. "I figured that if my own dad wouldn't bail me out, nobody would," he writes. "What a great lesson in being responsible for your actions."

Garry Trudeau, the creator of **Doonesbury,** told me that as a teenager in the 1930s, his father, Frank, went to Germany to watch the 1936 Berlin Olympics. When he ran out of cash before the games began, Frank sent a telegram to his father, asking him to wire money. I love the eight-word telegram his father sent back: DEAR FRANK. TOO BAD. SO SAD. LOVE DAD. Can you imagine a father responding that way today? Frank Trudeau stayed in Germany by borrowing money and finding odd jobs, and I have a feeling that, years later, he thanked his father for teaching him about responsibility.

President Jimmy Carter told me that, as a youngster, his main goal in life was to please his father, which he did by helping out on the family farm. His father used to call him "Hot," short for Hot Shot. One night, when the future president was twelve, his parents threw a party, with a lot of drinking and dancing that went on well into the night, keeping the youngster awake. Furious, he left the house and spent the night in his tree house. Shortly before dawn, his father noticed the boy was missing and started calling him. Jimmy didn't respond, but he snuck back into his room, where his father eventually found him.

"Why didn't you answer me when I called you?" his father asked.

"I don't know, Daddy."

That was one of about five times, by Carter's rough count, that his father gave him a whipping. This one hurt the most, he said, probably because his parents had been so worried when they couldn't find him. Commenting on his father's painful punishments, Carter said, "He only did it when I deserved it"—like the time he shot his sister in the butt with a BB gun. "But all of those whippings are memorable," he said. I would imagine so.

Times have changed, and I don't know any father who strikes his child. Still, there are times when a parent has to exercise a little discipline. One summer, when Luke missed curfew for a second time, I grounded him. But I realized that this punishment was inadequate and I had to do more to ensure that it wouldn't happen again. I drew up a contract that said if Luke came home late again, he would lose the use of his pickup truck for two weeks and would stay home for two consecutive weekends with no whining, no appeals, and no complaints. Luke signed it, and the deal held.

I'd love to claim credit for this idea, but it came from a conversation with Yankee shortstop Derek Jeter. Before every school year, Jeter told me, he would sit down with his parents and they would write up a document, outlining what they expected of him in school, on the playing field, and at home. And they would all sign it.

So was this your first contract? I asked him.

Yes, he said, and it was also the most difficult one to negotiate.

"And what would happen if you violated the terms of the deal?"

Referring to the signed document, he said, "You know, I was pretty good."

And he still is—the captain of the Yankees with a long-term contract.

THE PROPOSAL

There's an old movie cliché in which the brave commander slaps one of the recruits across the face, and the younger man says, "Thanks, I needed that." (It was also used in a commercial for Mennen aftershave.) Sometimes that slap is verbal, and sometimes that younger man is a full-grown adult.

When I finished college and Dad was driving me home, he said, "You're a little screwed up."

"What do you mean?"

"You've grown into a good-looking man, you have a strong back and a quick mind, but you worry too much about money."

"We never had any money, so of course I'm concerned about it. You don't know what it's like not being able to take my girlfriend to a movie or a dance."

"Well," he said, "don't worry about money. Worry about being the best at whatever you do. It may be hard for you to imagine, but we are miles better off than my parents." Then he said, "Hey, you ever seen a hearse with a luggage rack?"

In the next few years I was so focused on my career that I lost my wife, who had been my college sweetheart.

Dad said, "Looky here. Have you ever heard of the art of living? That's when you can't distinguish between a man at work or at play. By the way, how are your funds holding up?"

"Dad," I said, "I make almost twice as much as you."

"Yeah, I know," he said. "I just like to hear it."

I was twenty-seven when I met Jamie, an Ivy League beauty who loved me, and I loved her. But I was still snakebit from my first mistake, so I wanted to live with her before getting married. That was fine with Jamie, but my going-to-mass-twice-a-week mother was less than pleased. "You were raised better than that," Dad told me, "but listen, son, times are different. I'm not saying I condone what you are doing, but figure out what you need to figure out and I'll keep your mother at bay."

Two years later, when Jamie and I were living in Albuquerque and my parents were in Indianapolis, Dad called and said, "Tom, we need to talk. What's your Friday like?"

"It's open. What do you need?"

"Fly up here Friday morning and I'll meet you at the airport."

"How long should I stay?"

"This shouldn't take more than an hour. We'll talk at the airport, and you'll take the afternoon flight back. You're going to be busy this weekend."

When I got off the plane he was waiting for me. "Let's get down to business," he said. "You in or you out?"

"In or out with what?"

"With Jamie."

"Jamie's great."

"Terrific. When is the wedding?"

"Whoa, Dad. Who said anything about a wedding?"

"Look," said Dad, "I know that things are different than when I was your age, but when it comes to matters of the heart, not much has changed. Jamie's a beautiful young woman and your mother and I adore her, but that's not the point. You owe it to Jamie to be in or out. She's quite a gal, and she might be the mother of your kids someday. Treat her like it. You guys are young and have a lot on the ball. This country needs good families, not selfish young adults. So are you in or out?"

"Dad, I'm in, but why did you say I was going to be busy this weekend?"

"Well, if she says yes, you'll be out shopping for a diamond—trust me on that, kid. And if she says no, you'll be packing her up and putting a six-month deposit on a nice apartment for her."

"You want me to propose now?"

"I think your chances are better in person. Have a safe trip."

Eight months later we were married, and Dad was my best man. Six months later we took my parents on a vacation to Hawaii. Ten months after that, Dad died in his sleep.

—THOMAS A. BARR, Albuquerque, NM,
entrepreneur, son of
Jerome A. Barr, electric utility
manager (1925–1992)

THE BOARD

Why are kids so often surprised that it's not easy to put one over on the old man?

When we were about ten and twelve, my brother and I decided it was time to start smoking. But where would we hide the cigarettes? We found a loose board in the attic. Just the place, we thought, because the attic was a great venue. After all, nobody would smell smoke coming from the attic.

Two sons of a volunteer fireman smoking in the attic? Dumb and dumber! One evening, we decided it was time for a break in homework and a well-earned smoke, but much to our surprise—and horror—the loose floorboard was nailed shut. Nothing was ever said, or needed to be said. And we never smoked cigarettes again.

—MSGR. JOHN F. BENNETT,
Huntington, NY, pastor,
son of John J. Bennett,
postal employee (1904–1974)

THE ENFORCER

Talk about tough love—and not a word spoken.

In 1972 I was living with my parents in southern California, where our property included a house, a dairy barn, and several other small buildings. My sister and I were expected to utilize covered parking that was some distance from the house. Although I knew Dad's expectation, I continued to park my car in the shade of a peach tree near the house.

One morning, a couple of hours after Dad had left for work, I came out to hop in my little white bug to drive to classes. I noticed that the driver's side window had been rolled down, and that the biggest, thickest chain I had ever seen was connected to a huge padlock. It snaked around the trunk of the peach tree and through the window, effectively neutering my steering wheel and rendering the vehicle inoperable. I jumped on my bike and rode forty-five miles, round-trip, to make my classes that day, steaming all the way.

When I got home, the chain was still there. Dad didn't say a word about it, and neither did

I. The next morning it was gone, and you can bet I parked in the right spot from that day on.

—**Mitchell C. Thomas, Reno, NV, marriage and family therapist, son of Roy F. Thomas, building contractor (1919)**

THE ENVELOPE

I must have received at least twenty letters describing this type of enforced savings plan.

In the summer of 1968, I had just graduated from high school in Brooklyn and was eagerly awaiting the start of my college career at Brooklyn College in September. I got a summer job doing clerical work at a shipping company and made sixty dollars a week before taxes. When I told my father about the job, he was excited for me and added that he wanted me to contribute fifteen dollars a week for household expenses. I was angry at him for asking me to give up some of my hard-earned money, but I complied with his request every week.

The week before I started college, he handed me a large envelope that contained all the money I had given him over the summer. "I wasn't interested in your money," he told me. "I just wanted to teach you a little responsibility." And he did.

—IRA GERSHANSKY, Staten Island, NY, psychologist, son of Joseph Gershansky, bus maintainer (1914–1979)

THE ENGINEER

At work Dad created robots. At home he invented punishments. He seems to have been successful in both places.

I had a dad who read to me when Mom was too tired to think, a dad who knew when he walked in the door after a long day at work that Mom had had a tougher day at home, feeding and raising twelve children.

I had a dad who sacrificed so all of his children could attend Catholic schools. On Saturday nights, he used to line up our polished shoes so they would be ready for church on Sunday. He taught us by example. He came home from work every day, treated our mother with respect, and mopped the floors on his hands and knees.

This is the same man who made a robot that went to the moon, and who, in 1966, invented a surgical stapler that is used all over the world. Sometimes he would show home movies: We'd be watching a birthday party on the screen, and suddenly the scene would switch to an operating room. A dog was being operated on, and the surgeon would use Dad's staple gun rather than stitches to suture the poor animal. Then the scene would switch back to our family. Dad didn't bring much attention to himself—just to the object and its purpose.

Mom used to say that he could have achieved even more in his career, but he didn't want to uproot his family.

His creativity extended to punishments too. If you acted up, as we all did at times, you had to crack walnuts. (Dad would buy them in hundred-pound bags.) If you misbehaved in church, you had to kneel for forty-five minutes on our gravel driveway. When my oldest brother was fascinated with matches, Dad had him stand outside with a book of matches and light each one, holding it until it burned as far down as he could stand. If two of us were fighting, we had to stand in the kitchen, each in a separate square on the tile floor far enough apart so we couldn't reach each other, and think of three nice things about the other person. I use this form of discipline with my own kids.

The greatest legacy that Dad has left behind is that his children get along so well as adults. With all the sibling rivalry that existed as we were growing up, we still manage to get together often during the year, and we actually like one another. Dad taught us to care. In the long run, what more can a father do?

—JEANNE MORAN, teacher, Aledo, IL,
daughter of Jozef Slowik,
mechanical engineer (1922–2006)

The Survivor

"Pray to God, but row for shore."

—JOHN F. DESMOND,
father of
Mary Pinkowish

While serving in England during World War II, my dad was in a terrible airplane crash that put him in the hospital for six months with bad burns and a broken jaw. Other men, of course, were even less fortunate. Many didn't return at all, and of those who did, some came home with disfigurements, missing limbs, or severe emotional problems. Stan Baryza, who lived three doors from us, had been a sergeant in the U.S. Army's 76th Infantry Division. After he was wounded in Germany, his leg was amputated six inches below the knee. He walked with a limp, and as his neighbors, we saw another grim reminder of his injury: Every family hung its wash on the line, and the Baryzas' laundry included a woolen stump sock—a very long sock that went over what remained of Stan Baryza's left leg.

Mr. Baryza worked as a tool and dye inspector and studied to be an optician, but he refused to let his disability limit him. Like many dads in our neighborhood, he was always working on or around the house: shoveling the driveway, climbing a ladder to put up the storm windows, or cleaning out the gutters. He was also our Boy Scout troop leader, and we were a rowdy bunch. As far as we knew, he never complained. The only concession he ever made, his son, Fran, told me recently, was that he wouldn't put on a bathing suit. "We grew up thinking that every dad had an artificial leg," Fran added, and I learned from some of the letters that this was true in other families as well. We knew that Mr. Baryza had a disability, but we didn't think of him as disabled or as someone to feel sorry for.

Some dads carry the burden of war wounds. Others are weighed down by alcoholism, cancer, heart disease, or other infirmities. Brad Reardon's father needed a new liver, and his son's account of how he provided it appears in this chapter. Around the time Reardon's letter came in, I heard from a colleague of Kate Drohan, the women's softball coach at Northwestern University, and of Kate's identical twin sister, Caryl, the associate head coach. Back in 1984, their father, John, a retired New York fireman, underwent a heart transplant. At the time, John knew that he had only a 50 percent chance of seeing his twin daughters reach their teenage years. "Actually," Kate told me in a letter, "he didn't live to **watch** his kids grow up. He lived to **help** us grow up."

In September 2004, John Drohan needed a second transplant—a kidney this time, because of the side effects of the drugs he had been taking ever since his heart transplant. The waiting list for a cadaver donor was two years, but John didn't have that long. There were plenty of volunteers within the family who were willing to donate a kidney, including John's two sons, but they didn't "match." Kate and Caryl both did.

Each daughter wanted to be the one to donate a kidney, and they argued about it for days. The skills of compromise that they had developed over thirty years did not apply here. Although they listened to each other's questions, such as, "How would the person feel who didn't do it?" or "What if something happened to one of us?" neither twin would give in. Through it all, their primary concern was, What if it didn't work?

Finally, unable to decide, they asked a friend to flip a coin, which was how this unusual honor fell to Kate. After the operation, Caryl told her sister that despite everything their dad had just been through, all he seemed to care about was that Kate was all right. When they were reunited in the recovery room, he embraced his daughter and said, "What's the matter? You look a little tired." That, says Kate, was his way of saying thanks.

Kate's surgery took three hours and left her with a five-inch scar on her stomach. But she doesn't have to stay on any medicine, and she was told that her life expectancy was not affected. "Of course that sounds funny to me," she says, "because I know from my father that my scientific life expectancy is probably not accurate anyway. Besides, I suspect Dad would have you know that it's more important to be concerned about your life's impact than its length." I have never met John Drohan, but he must be a hell of a father.

THE RIDE

Sometimes a dying dad will hang on if there's something to live for. And there was. And he did.

My father was a first-generation Italian-American, and I was his only son. All my sisters had married and given him grandchildren, and he was as content as he could be, considering that his dear Gracie, my mother, had been dead five years. He seemed resigned to the fact that, having hit forty, I would probably never marry and give him a grandchild.

Then I met a lovely woman, and after a short time we were married. Within months, Pop was diagnosed with metastatic liver and lung cancer. Upon hearing the news that he had less than a year, he bravely said that he wasn't afraid to die. Then Marie and I found out that we were expecting. I went to tell Pop, but when I got to his house he was sleeping—knocked out from the chemotherapy. I sat and waited, but he soon awoke and sensed that something was up. When I told him the news, he sat up and said, "I'm gonna make that."

It wasn't easy. He was taking chemo through his chest from a portable machine. Some days, when I'd phone him, he would just whisper "Bad day" and hang up.

On the day our daughter was born, as soon as my wife and child were safely tucked in at the maternity ward, I drove to tell Dad. His eyes opened from a deep sleep. He smiled and said, "Tell me." When I did, he sat up and clapped as hard as he could. Before he drifted off, I managed to say that my new family would visit as soon as possible.

Early the next morning the phone rang in my wife's hospital room. My sister Theresa said that she and Pop were on their way. I tried to tell her that the long ride would be a torment for Pop, but she said he was already in the car and wouldn't get out until he reached the hospital. An hour and a half later, they arrived. When I opened his car door, Pop woke up and said, "Let's go see our little doll."

Dad's legs were really weak from the trip, so I got him a wheelchair and up we went. When he got to Marie's room, Dad asked me to bring the baby to him, saying that he couldn't hold her because his arms were too tired. He told me to put her up near his face, then he leaned over, kissed her, and said, "Sheila Mary, Grandpa loves you very much."

Theresa took a picture of my daughter, me, and Dad, the only picture that exists of my dad with any of my children. Within seconds, Pop was asleep. He woke up as we were helping him into the car. I told him how sorry I was that he had to go through so much, including over three hours in a car, for a ten-minute visit. He smiled. "Danny, if it was only a minute, it was worth it!" As they drove away I cried uncontrollable tears of joy.

Dad's days after that were not many. My sister Olympia said Pop knew his work was done; we were all on our way with our own families. My daughters often ask me to tell them the story of Mommy in the hospital, and Grandpa's great gift of unconditional love.

In time, we have come to understand the fruits of this gift—how to be lifegiving even when you're drained of physical energy; the dignity of spirit in accepting your limitations; giving affection, which can be as simple as putting your lips on a baby's cheek; and grace in the words that Pop shared with his son, who was watching one life end as another was beginning.

—Dan Mazzeo, Bridgehampton, NY,
home health aide, son of
John Mazzeo, auto mechanic
(1924–1994)

THE DINNER

"When he wasn't drinking"—how much hope and fear is squeezed into those four words.

We had our moments, my father and I. He was an alcoholic who somehow never missed a day's work at Bethlehem Steel in Sparrows Point, Maryland. (When I was growing up, I thought everyone's father worked "down the Point.")

When he wasn't drinking, he was a good man—intelligent, compassionate, and witty. When he drank, he was dark and abusive. I frequently awoke to loud arguments, dishes being smashed against the wall, my mother screaming in the dead of night. I lay in bed, a skinny little girl paralyzed with fear.

There were separations over the years, but she always took him back. There were bad, bad memories to be sure. But then there was that Christmas!

It was 1966. I was sixteen and a junior in high school. The steel plant had had a major layoff. Dad was out of work, and we were out of money. My father was sober and had been for several days. But a thick tension hovered over us, and I waited all day for the explosion.

We sat down to eat around five o'clock, just the three of us, as I was an only child. Things were so bad we were having scrambled eggs for Christmas dinner! In my mind's eye, I could envision those eggs eventually ending up on the wall.

As I pulled my chair closer to the table, my father stood up. In the silence, he looked at my mother for what seemed an eternity. Then he picked up a carving knife and a fork, leaned over the eggs, and with a perfectly serious face looked at me and asked, "Would you like a breast or thigh?"

I responded, "A thigh, please, and some of that delicious dressing."

Just like that, in a magical moment he had diffused the tension. This man who had so many faces, who could rip the phone out of the wall because I was talking too long, but who might wake up early the next morning so he could polish my shoes for church—this man who would strike my mother one night, but the next afternoon take all the money he had been saving up to buy himself an air conditioner and come back instead with an engagement ring to replace the one she had lost—this man had turned a corner.

It was the richest Christmas of my life. He died the following year.

—PATRICIA MAY, retired teacher,
Baltimore, MD, daughter of
Oliver "Terry" Tereo,
steelworker (1923–1967)

THE BACHELOR'S FATHER

I can't help but wonder: How many of those women did he meet before he made his decision?

Losing doesn't build character; it reveals it. Although my father's life has taken many turns, the word **loser** seems to have followed him around. He grew up in the Depression-era Bronx with little money. He had a famous older brother, Dolph Schayes, who was one of the fifty greatest NBA players, but he wasn't able to equal his brother's success.

My father was drafted into the army during the time he planned to try out for the NBA. He played for the Washington Generals (who were known overseas as the Texas Cowboys), the main foils of the Harlem Globetrotters, which meant losing over two thousand games without a single victory. Later, he managed bowling alleys and drugstores to provide for his family, and finally, at seventy, he started caring for patients who had been branded as losers.

He used to tell me that losing two thousand games did not make him a loser. He refused to be defined by what a scoreboard said.

My father was a survivor, not a loser. He worked hard, six days a week, to provide for his family. I call him a hero.

At my bar mitzvah, I told my dad he was my best friend and would be my best man at my wedding. As time went by, I didn't find anyone to marry, and I forgot my promise to

Dad. Twenty-three years went by, and I finally met somebody in 2001 by holding up a sign in Hebrew at the Maccabiah Games in Israel: SINGLE AMERICAN MAN SEEKING ISRAELI WIFE. CONTACT TODD SCHAYES AT THE TEL AVIV HILTON. Over six thousand women responded, and one of them became my wife. And I remembered my promise. I called Dad, told him I was getting married, and asked if he would be my best man. There was no answer on the other end of the line. My mom finally came on the phone and said, "Your father is in the other room crying."

—TODD SCHAYES, Greenwood Village, CO, teacher, basketball coach, son of Herman Schayes, hospital aide (1933)

THE GIFT

Talk about giving of yourself!

This is the phone call I hoped would never come. My stepmother's voice shudders through tears to tell me something is wrong. It is nearly impossible to make out what she is saying, but it must be about my father. For a minute I believe he is dead, and I fall to the floor of my apartment. I'm not ready for this.

After calming down a bit, she says he is now in stable condition. The night before his temperature had soared to 104 degrees, and he was rushed to the emergency room. We all knew that a night like this was inevitable.

It had been almost a decade since he was told he would need a liver transplant. When he was diagnosed with ulcerative colitis in his late twenties, his doctor prescribed the steroid Prednisone. But the dosage was not monitored closely enough, and the drug did irreparable damage to his liver.

A few months after that night at the hospital he was placed on a transplant list for a cadaver liver, one of thousands waiting for a stranger's death to give them new life. While he tried to convince me that this was the best solution, my own research showed most people don't survive the wait. I also learned about live-liver donation.

After some long conversations, my father realized that I would never relent until he agreed to let me give him half of my liver. He had lost his father to heart disease when he was five, and his mother to cancer when he was twenty. His parents had died young and he had been powerless to help them, but I had a unique opportunity to do more than sit helplessly at his bedside.

For our family, the operation was twelve hours of agony. The doctors found a blood clot in the portal vein leading to his liver, which nearly doubled the surgery time and required a major blood transfusion. Had they found the clot before starting the surgery, the procedure would have been canceled. Permanently.

The following spring, my father was at my graduation. Two years after that, he was dancing at my wedding. It has been nearly five years since the surgery and we both feel great, although his days of beating me at H-O-R-S-E have long since passed. He gave me the gift of life, and twenty-three years later I was able to give it back.

—**BRAD REARDON, Seattle, WA, writer, son of Tim Reardon, attorney (1948)**

THE SCULPTOR

He could have been a victim, but he made a different choice.

He wasn't a hero. He was simply a hardworking, dedicated, and loving father. He had already given us the greatest gift a father can give his children—the unlimited love of our mother.

He worked two jobs to feed the family and get us through our nonnegotiable education. Then, in the spring of 1963, he was shot through the head by juvenile thugs, leaving him blind.

Until that evening, my mother's full-time job had been raising her boys. Our full-time job was getting the best grades we could, so we could become professionals.

In his blindness we now judged my father differently. Suddenly he was a hero. He announced almost immediately that he was inconvenienced rather than handicapped. Depression can be contagious, and he was determined to restrict his worst feelings to his private moments. In public he fell back on his Myron Cohen–like sense of humor, which was pretty good; in his youth, he had worked in

the Catskills as a singer and comedian. But
now his repertoire included some funny stories about his blindness.

When people asked him, as they often did,
"Sam, is it true that when you lose your sight,
your other senses improve?" our dad would always answer the question with a hand cupped
over his ear and a loud "**What?**" He just made
people feel comfortable.

He loved to tell the neighbors that his two
college sons had given him a color TV for their
parents' fortieth anniversary, when we had actually given him a Braille watch and our
mother the TV. The neighbors believed him,
and we played along.

At family events, he always brought the
house down by singing "Sunrise, Sunset," followed by "Because of You," dedicated to our
mother, with a curtain call of "My Way." He
taught us to laugh at ourselves, live in the present, and express our love both verbally and
with hugs. My brother and I never let a day go
by without calling, not just to check in but because we enjoyed every conversation. Our
wives loved him as if he were their own father,
and in our marriages we have emulated his
complete devotion and love.

He became a stone sculptor, using only touch and imagination, and even sold a few pieces. He learned how to package photographic paper in an environment of total darkness, and he was always faster than the sighted employees. He learned to take the subway to Manhattan and was the star at the Vacation Camp for the Blind for two weeks each summer, where he organized a diving contest with blind judges. But that's a whole other story.

My brother and I have never lived more than a mile apart, another testament to his teaching of family values. Our father is gone now, and we miss speaking to him every day. He was like vitamins for the spirit.

—ALAN WASSERSTEIN, Morganville, NJ,
marketing executive, son of
Sam Wasserstein, garment worker
(1913–1978)

THE DISABILITY

**We've all heard about the man who was
sad because he had no shoes—until he
met a man who had no feet. It's hard not
to think about that line when you read
this.**

When I was seven, I was sitting at our kitchen
table asking my father how I could be born
with two legs if he only had one. "I was born
with two legs too," he replied, "but an accident took one away." His voice was clear and
gentle, but he didn't elaborate. My mother was
quiet. My younger sister, Nancy, swayed her
head back and forth in wide-eyed observation.
It was said, and it was accepted.

In 1944, Ed D'Amico went off to war and
lost his right leg. The accident occurred in the
pit of a gun mount aboard the USS **St. Paul**
during an unscheduled exercise of the weapon.
I was in my late teens before he really talked
about it, maybe because that was a more appropriate age to begin to understand such a
loss. Or perhaps it was because Dad's lost limb
was almost irrelevant.

His attitude never betrayed his eternal optimism and zest for life. After the accident, he was hospitalized at naval facilities in Hawaii, Oakland, and Philadelphia for recovery and rehabilitation. He looked around him for months and saw many young men with no legs, or no arms, and men with no limbs at all. He felt lucky. He went home after a year and turned his entire disability pay over to his parents for six years, helping them support his nine siblings until he married my mother. Ed D'Amico was a doer; actions fueled his dreams. My parents saved diligently and built a home. They raised three girls. Dad had two jobs for a long time so he could give us special things, modest vacations, and, later on, help us with college tuition. Frugality, born of necessity when he was younger, evolved into a virtue. Dad mowed his own lawn, maintained and repaired our cars, unearthed large rocks in the woods to build stone walls around the property, and even reroofed the house. No one ever thought of Ed D'Amico as handicapped at all.

—DOREEN D'AMICO, Sarasota, FL,
loan officer, daughter of
Edward A. D'Amico,
lab technician (1926–1998)

THE BANKER

A dad who decided that freedom meant more than power.

If it hadn't been for my dad, our whole family would still be in Cuba. He was a successful attorney when Fidel Castro declared himself Marxist-Leninist less than a year after taking over. Within six months, Dad was offered a cabinet post in the new Castro government. Dad flatly rejected it, although he knew his refusal would mean losing everything he had built over the course of twenty-five years. (He was fifty at the time.)

One night in the summer of 1960, Dad gathered the family around the dinner table and told us we would be leaving the country immediately. He had my plane ticket ready, and he told me that as the oldest—I was twenty-one—I would leave first, together with my brother-in-law, to establish a beachhead for the family in the United States. Dad, my mother, my two sisters, my younger brother, and my wife would follow as soon as we found a place to live and some means of sustenance.

Dad left no room for discussion. He put some one- and five-dollar bills on the dining room table, together with toothpaste tubes, small plastic bags, and packs of cigarettes. Then he led us in rolling the bills and squeezing them into the empty toothpaste tubes and cigarettes. We spent three days and nights doing this. I don't know what my dad had to do to secure the necessary traveling papers and tickets for the whole family. What I do know is that Dad left behind everything he had built up from a middle-class lifestyle over three decades.

All our lives, Dad had told us again and again that he would help us get the best education he could possibly provide. He also told us that material wealth might come and go, and that our real inheritance would be our education. When my brother-in-law and I left Cuba, I carried thirty dollars in American money in toothpaste tubes and cigarettes—and, of course, my education. Dad's last words when he took us to the airport were **"Julio, para atrás, ni para tomar impulso"**—Julio, never take a step back, not even to gather momentum.

Dad couldn't practice law in the United States, but that didn't stop him. He went to work for a bank in New York City, making less money than I, his twenty-one-year-old son, who was selling life insurance to make ends meet while going to college at night. Over the course of the next thirty-seven years, Dad, who came over with fifty dollars, became president of one of the country's largest banks. His honesty and straightforwardness became legendary in his industry, exactly as it had been in Cuba, which was why Castro had wanted to rub himself with some of Dad's impeccable reputation. During these years, Dad has seen fifteen grandchildren and seventeen great-grandchildren come to life in America. And we, his children, learned the lesson he so determinedly ingrained in us. Every one of his fifteen grandchildren is a college graduate.

—JULIO J. CASTELLANOS, Valencia, CA,
international management, retired,
son of Julio J. Castellanos, attorney (1910)

THE REUNION

Dads can change. It doesn't happen all that often, but when it does, what a blessing!

I grew up in Florida, and a few years after my parents divorced, my dad moved to Tennessee to remarry. We stayed in touch for a while and I visited him a few times, but we gradually lost contact with each other. I heard that he had been drinking and was going through some hard times.

About seven years after I had last seen him, I was driving with my young daughter when I nearly hit a man who was crossing the street. I recognized him and turned around, screaming for him to stop. He looked scared until he recognized me. The initial contact was very uncomfortable, but we shared a hug and set a time to meet the next day.

When we met, my father told me that he had been back in Florida for a while, living in a rooming house. Although he didn't say so explicitly, I had the impression that he had been too ashamed to call. I visited with him as much as I could and the years seemed to melt away, but he was still drinking and had other problems. Unfortunately, I didn't have much time for him: I had a heavy college load and was working full time as a paramedic, so I urged him to go back to Tennessee, where his sister and other family members could care for him. It took some persuading, but he finally agreed to go. His sister arranged for him to have a complete physical for the first time in years, and my father got himself into a twelve-step program.

My dad has been sober for ten years and has spoken for numerous twelve-step programs throughout Tennessee. He has beaten prostate cancer and serves on the town board. He spends his time driving people to doctors' appointments and helping out in his community.

He has taught me that no matter how bad things get, and whether or not it's your fault, you can bounce back and become a positive influence on yourself, your family, and your community.

—TIM ARNWINE, Pembroke Pines, FL,
business owner, son of
Ray Arnwine, community
volunteer (1936)

THE OPTIMIST

So many fathers had every reason to be depressed. Especially this one.

At eighty-five, my father could have been a poster child for healthy aging. He was avid about his hobbies, read everything he could get his hands on, and jogged four miles a day. He and my mother also had an active social life.

Then he was diagnosed with malignant melanoma. Despite his age, he instructed his doctors to take all possible measures to prolong his life. Whatever the treatment was, he said, if it would give him more time with his grandchildren, he was willing to undergo it.

Shortly after his first surgery, I accompanied him to the hospital for follow-up tests. We were sitting next to each other in a long line of chairs in a noisy corridor, waiting to be called for blood work. We had chatted in the car, but now we were silent. In response to nothing, he said, "You know, I've had a very good life. True, I was in a concentration camp for five years and lost my first wife and child, but all in all I've had a very happy life."

What could I say? He did have a happy life because he believed he did. I put my hand on his and we waited quietly together.

—SHARON SAMET, New Rochelle, NY, social worker, daughter of Imre Samet, businessman (1913–1999)

Let Me Tell You a Little About Him

"My father never preached very much. He just let me watch him lead his life."

—MIKE HESS, son of Bernard Hess

A few years ago, well before I ever imagined writing a book about Big Russ, I used to pay tribute to him whenever I was asked to give a commencement address. At first I thought it was impossible to describe, in just a few words, how important my father was to me, but when I really thought about it I came up with this: "He taught me more by the quiet eloquence of his hard work . . . by his basic decency . . . by his intense loyalty. . . . He taught me the true lessons of life."

Every time I spoke those words to college graduates and their parents, I could feel a tug—not only in my own heart but in the collective heart of the audience, which was often expressed by a murmur of appreciation for **their** fathers. People would come up to me after the speech to say, "You know, that's exactly how I feel about **my** dad."

As I read through the thousands of letters that came in, some of them quite lengthy, from time to time a line or two caught my eye for its power, its beauty, or its originality. These comments may be brief, but they tell us so much about individual fathers and the huge impact they had on their grateful sons and daughters. Whether it's something these fathers said or the way they lived, these are some of the memories, the legacies, and the wisdom they passed on.

My dad taught me to tie my shoes, to cross the street, to get an education, and to believe in my country, my God, and my family. I never had to look far for my hero. He was just across the living room, sitting in his favorite chair, reading the newspaper and watching the nightly news.

—**Dixie Wilson, daughter of Carl Wilson Jr., machinist**

Dad was honest—Abe Lincoln honest.

—**Dave Esto, son of Donald James Esto, plant foreman**

Dad's been gone three years now, but I still think of him every day—the way he would laugh at a joke so hard that he'd start to cry, or how, when we were little, he'd get up in the morning, come down for breakfast, and remind us to say good morning to Mr. Sun. All these years later, I finally realized: **He** was the sun.

—**REBECCA BLOCKER, daughter of
Donald Blocker, salesman**

My father embodied a remark by Winston Churchill: "We make a living by what we get, but we make a life by what we give."

—**CHRISTINE A. SMITH, daughter of
Francis D. Smith, detective**

My dad was a rail rider, a risk taker, a joke teller, and a blue-eyed twinkling package of humor, love, and compassion.

—**CATHY CONAWAY, daughter of
Russell Hanstrom, businessman**

My father once told me that by the time he was seven, he had stopped drinking coffee and smoking cigarettes. It cracks me up to think he had given up his bad habits by the age of seven. My dad—the infantile delinquent.

—**JUDY KISAILUS, daughter of
Steve Trubilla, welder**

When I was nineteen and an honors student at journalism school, I told my parents I was gay. My father put me in a mental institution. Yes, you could do that back in 1974. He wanted me to be cured, but it didn't work at all, which was quite a shock to Mr. Phi Beta Kappa.

Ten years later, the very same man flew two thousand miles to sit in the front row during opening night of a gay play I had written. He applauded with gusto and was charming and sweet at the cast party. This is what fathers do for us. So many of them will bridge any chasm to connect with us.

—JIM BLOOR, son of Robert Bloor, chemist

After my divorce, my father advised me to always pay my bills on time to keep my credit good, always have money in the bank, and always wear a bra.

—CARLA DALE, daughter of Mike Foschi, factory supervisor

Sometimes I find myself offering this prayer: "Please don't let me give up on my son, as my father didn't give up on his."

—MIKE SCHACTER, son of
Irving Schacter, retailer

A couple of years ago I called to congratulate my parents on their fifty-third wedding anniversary, and I complimented them on how much their marriage has meant to their children. As I was shedding a tear, Dad said, "That's a load of baloney. The deal between your mother and me was that whoever left first had to take all eight of you!"

—DON SMITH JR., son of Don Smith Sr.,
manufacturing supervisor

Had my dad lived long enough for me to learn to express myself, I would have loved to let him know how much he meant to me.

—AL ZUSMAN, son of Benjamin Zusman,
sportswriter

He taught me the importance of a solid hand-shake, the disarming ability of relevant small talk, and the unmistakable effectiveness and success that comes from treating people fairly.

—**THOMAS J. MCKEEVER, son of Timothy J. McKeever, manager**

I was never a stepchild, only a loved child.

—**MICHELE THOMPSON, daughter of Peter Mariluch, retired banker**

My father's life would not make chapter one of anyone's book, but he taught me how to live by the way **he** lived. He worked hard, loved his family, had integrity, and wouldn't compromise his values. He wasn't famous, and he didn't have a lot of material things—just character and backbone, society's missing links.

—**SUSAN W. JONES, daughter of Walter B. Watson, road master**

The year before my father died, I took him to the local Fourth of July parade. For many years in the past he had walked the parade route as a member of a club that supported the celebration. That year, however, we sat on folding lawn chairs and just watched.

When the first band approached with flags flying, Dad struggled out of his lawn chair and put his hat over his heart. Then the next band came by—and the same struggle. After the third or fourth band, I had to tell him to just forget it. He was incredulous. This was the flag of his country, he reminded me. "How can I not at least stand up?"

—SANDRA JOHAN, daughter of
Elmer DeFazio, dentist

I was my father's princess. Growing up in a rural area of the Deep South could have been a harsh experience for a little black girl, but I was insulated by his love and tenderness.

—GLENDA BOYD, daughter of
Donald Starr, educator

We have an interesting dynamic, my pop and I. I call him a greedy and heartless SOB and he calls me a commie-socialist-knee-jerk-pinko liberal. These are terms of endearment in our family.

We have completely opposite views of the world, but his guidance and openness about life have led me to form my own views and helped shape the woman I am and will become. I find myself speaking often of my father to people who don't know him, as if in order to understand me they need to know about him.

—FRANCES BOYES, daughter of Michael Boyes, bagel shop owner

You can't legislate profound and intrinsic decency and integrity, but you can encourage it. And, as I've been fortunate enough to observe by watching my father, you can exemplify it.

—THOMAS D. LeFEVRE, son of David A. LeFevre, chemical engineer

I grew in stature simply by standing near my dad.

—BURTON YALOWICH, son of Rubin Yalowich, pharmacist

My father was one of those special people who come along in life who make you feel better just by being there.

—TOM AKERS, son of Ray Akers Sr., funeral director

"Good morning, Dad. How are you today?"
"I am alive and that's enough."

—ROSY RODRIGUEZ, daughter of Raul Rodriguez, plant manager

My dad always taught us that nobody is better than you are, and you aren't better than anyone else.

—**Michele Licata Gallo, daughter of Julio A. Licata, drugstore clerk**

He has always been my gentle critic and my biggest fan.

—**Randall Adams, son of Woodrow Adams, coal miner**

My father valued a discount or a sale almost as much as his religion. When he passed, I wanted to put on his headstone, "I did not bargain for this." Sadly, but perhaps wisely, my family vetoed the suggestion. But he would have loved it.

—**Peter Cove, son of Sam Cove, salesman**

At my father's funeral, the minister said, "Jack Kendall didn't wear his heart on his sleeve because his sleeve wasn't big enough."

—**Brad Kendall, son of Jack Kendall, banker**

My dad was hard of hearing and didn't like using his hearing aids. When I was in high school, I said, "Dad, can you give me five bucks?"

He said, "What? I didn't hear you."

"I need ten bucks."

"Be quiet," he said. "I heard you the first time."

What goes around, comes around. I find that I, too, have developed selective hearing loss.

—**LLOYD BURGENER**, son of
Lloyd Burgener, farmer

Pop was dependable, and he expected the same from me. He would often say, "People are counting on you," which was his way of encouraging both timeliness and honesty.

—**DUANE V. ACKERMAN**, son of
Dallas G. Ackerman, plant manager

He was always able to make the hard times easier and the good times better.

—**ROBERT BAKER**, son of
Dave Baker, farmer

My father cut hair six days a week for forty-five years. That's all he ever did, and all he ever knew. He provided for my mom, my three brothers, and me by saying, "How short do you want it?"

—MICHAEL CARUSO, son of
Nicholas Caruso, barber

It seems that some people are destined to sacrifice more than they ever receive in return, and all we can do is wonder at their generosity.

—BRIAN PLACKIS CHENG, son of
Constantine N. Plackis, telecom executive

My father worked hard and saw that as his mission. He brought home the bacon, and every slice counted.

—DOROTHY NELSON, daughter of
E. H. Pederson, retail manager

Whenever I called him I would say, "Hi, Dad, this is Kathie," and he would respond, "Kathie who?"

"Kathie your daughter."

"Which one?"

"Your one and only."

"Oh, that one!"

No matter what he was doing, we always had this banter. It made me feel special, because he didn't care who was listening or how important they were. I was more important.

—**Kathie Decker, daughter of Robert M. Hurley, architect**

There has never been a man who worked so hard for so long, and ended up with so little, as my dad.

—**Felicia J. Swisher, daughter of Frederick G. Sullivan, home construction**

If my father were alive, I would want to thank him for not reminding me of the arrogance and narcissism that I exhibited during my college years. Isn't it interesting how much smarter our fathers become after **we** have finished our formal education?

—**Robert Vogel, son of Vernon Vogel, electrical engineer**

Dad was diagnosed with cancer in 1981, and he waged a war that I was sure he would win. During the four years that he lived with cancer, he traveled with Mom, saw three of his children get married, and welcomed several grandchildren. He was a strong man who didn't like to ask for help, which led one of the priests in our parish to remind Dad, "We're supposed to imitate Christ, not outdo Him."

—Donna Pizzolongo, daughter of
George E. Raboni Sr., attorney

My father would fantasize about winning millions in the lottery, and would sit down and make a list of every person he would give it away to. He always left himself out. My mom would say, "Harry, what about us?" And he would answer, "Mary, we don't need anything. We have our house paid off, plenty of food on the table, and we don't owe anybody any money. What more could we want?"

—Linda Raviele, daughter of
Harry Raviele, sanitation worker

Father Knows Best

"When I was a boy, my father was boss. Now that I'm a dad, my son is boss. When do I get to be boss?"

—WILLIAM H. J. MURRAY, father of William J. Murray

Like many fathers, my dad has a few favorite expressions. When I was a boy, and he thought I was overly impressed with myself, he would say, "Don't get too big for your britches." At a restaurant, he would ask the waitress for the check by saying, "What's the damage?" At supper, he would sometimes tell us, "What you hear at this table stays at this table," although I can't remember any real secrets ever being disclosed. But his favorite expression has always been, "What a country!" It means so many things: how fortunate we are, what a great hot dog this is, how much opportunity and upward mobility America provides, and, quite literally, what a great country we live in.

In my previous book, I quoted another of Big Russ's favorite expressions: "You gotta eat!" As soon as the book was published, he called to tell me that I had it wrong. "I got that from Dr. Matty Burke," he told me, "but you forgot the second part. 'You gotta eat—if you're gonna drink!' "

No matter how many conversations we have with our dads, they often boil down to a few choice words that seem to define him, or a single line that etches itself into our memory. Some of these sayings are original, others have a time-honored history, but to the sons and daughters who remember these words, they will always belong to their dads.

The only place where success comes before work is in the dictionary.

—HERMAN SCHAYES, coach,
hospital aide

Do what you have to do first, and what you want to do second.

—DONALD JARVIS,
shop supervisor

Be a good listener. Sometimes when you just sit and listen, the other person will answer his own question and will thank you for your help.

—RUSSELL FOGLESONG, sales

Go for broke. What's the worst that can happen? If they say no, you're right back where you started. And they might say yes.

—RAY HASSON, TV producer

Get to know and show respect for clerks and secretaries, because they are the gatekeepers.

—DONALD MCCARTHY, attorney

Don't let other people's actions govern yours.

—JEAN SMITH, railroad yardmaster

If you ever get taken to jail, don't waste your one phone call calling home.

—JAMES W. GEORGE, chef

Save your employer enough money to cover your salary each year.

—HAROLD ROBERT CHATTAWAY,
computer programmer

What you are to be, you are now becoming.

—RUSSEL LESTER SNYDER, artist

Choose good friends. If you walk past garbage, you will smell like garbage.

—EMILIO SAPORITO, dye-house worker

Nobody ever paid me not to go to work.

—HOMER MORRISEY, farmer

Don't brag. It's not the whistle that pulls the train.

—NAT LANDAU, **insurance salesman**

Procrastination is the thief of time.

—GEORGE F. NEWELL, **educator**

Never replace just one spark plug.

—LESTER WILLIAM DREYER, **steamfitter**

The fruit you reach for is better than the fruit that falls at your feet.

—CLYDE SMITH, **transportation operator**

Drive with care. Life has no spare.

—BERNARD GOTTLIEB, **businessman**

You've never gone so far down the wrong road that you can't turn around.

—DAVID A. LEFEVRE, **chemical engineer**

If you work with your hands, you will never go hungry.

—SALVATORE N. GERACI, **chef**

If you can't combine business with pleasure, go out of business.

—NORMAN C. CLARK, foreman

Son, do you see those betting windows? Look at how many of them sell tickets, and how many cash out tickets for the winners. What does that tell you?

—HARRY MAZIAR, businessman

Practice hard. You'll play the way you practiced.

—NICK COSMOS, coach

When a young son saw Sophia Loren on TV and asked his father why he hadn't married her: Because I met your mother first.

—JAMES DONALD CURRY, farmer

If I can just have enough money to educate my kids with enough left to bury me when I die, I will be a happy man.

—GEORGE REASOR,
railroad repairman

Life is a succession of freshman years.

—GENE "CLARK" KALHORN,
business owner

If you're going to hoot with the owls, you have to soar with the eagles.

—HARRY F. KELLY JR., public relations

A clear conscience is a soft pillow.

—HARRY DAVID LaVENTURE, shirt cutter

We all can't be lighthouses. Some of us have to be candles.

—HARRY GELLER, barber

Be grateful that I'm still yelling at you, because that means I still care. When I don't say anything—that's when you should worry.

—WILLIAM PRAMBERGER,
financial analyst

We are often broke, but we have never been poor.

—JOSEPH KEITH MILLER,
shoe salesman

If you got something you didn't work for, then someone else worked for something they didn't get.

—JOE DAN PRADO, banker

You can never be perfect. But the harder you try, the closer you'll come.

—JOHN VALENTINE BARCZAK, salesman

If you could buy him for what he knows and sell him for what he thinks he knows, you'd turn quite a profit.

—MARCUS L. BEMENT, paint mixer

The title of **boyfriend** means nothing in this house.

—RICHARD J. QUIGLEY, IT executive

Don't be so heavenly minded that you're no earthly good.

—DALLAS G. ACKERMAN, plant manager

You'd be amazed what you can do when you have to.

—JAMES JOSEPH VAUGHAN, operating engineer

A lucky man gets up in the morning, knows what he has to do, and thinks it still matters.

—Joe Biden Sr., salesman

If things get tight and you can't pay both your car loan and your mortgage, be sure to pay the car loan first. You can live in your car, but you can't drive your house.

—Frank Pennella, carpenter

Don't ruin a holiday. You can always fight tomorrow. Once the holiday is gone, you can't get it back.

—George E. Raboni Sr., attorney

A laboring man's rest is sweet, and I always slept well.

—James E. Hill, street sweeper, truck driver

Epilogue

"I will always be here for you. We are bonded by blood."
—TIM RUSSERT, son of Tim "Big Russ" Russert, father of Luke Russert

Sometimes the hardest part of being a father are the things you can't say. In the early fall of 2004, as Luke prepared to go off to college, I was excited for him. My own college experience had been deeply satisfying; I loved my new independence, enjoyed my courses, made new friends, and became head of the club that brought a number of big-name rock groups to campus. Now Luke would have his own chance to grow more independent and pursue his passion for living and, I hope, learning.

But as the day grew closer when Maureen and I would take him to college, I became increasingly sad. Luke was my son, and I would miss having him home, but he was also my friend and my companion, and I would miss him in those roles as well. We had gone to countless ball games together, and on Sunday afternoons during the football season he would usually join me on the couch to watch the Buffalo Bills on satellite TV. How could I ever get used to not having him there?

Ever since he had learned to drive he had become increasingly independent, but even then, he still lived with us, and there was always the comfort of knowing that he was upstairs sleeping, that he was **around.** I knew his going to college didn't mean the end of our relationship—he would come home from time to time, and we could talk on the phone and on e-mail, and Maureen and I would soon be going back to Boston for parents' weekend—but my heart was aching over his imminent absence.

When departure day arrived, the three of us flew to Boston. We took Luke to his dorm room and helped set it up. Then, when there was nothing left to do, Maureen and I just stood there, both of us unwilling to leave. Luke thanked us for everything and gently suggested that it was time to say good-bye. We each gave him a hug. I hesitated, wondering if I should give him a letter I had written, but instead I hugged him again and slipped him a couple of twenties.

A moment after we left, I went back in and handed him an envelope. "Here," I said, "I want you to have this."

"What is it?"

"Read it when I leave."
"No, wait, I'll read it now."

Dear Luke,
Off you go.
New school. New city. New friends. New challenges.
You are more than ready. Whether it was New York or Washington; West Side Montessori, St. Columba's, Beauvoir, or St. Albans, you connected with people and made your mark.
I've so enjoyed watching and helping you grow. We've had an amazing nineteen years together. I hope we have at least another nineteen!
I will always be here for you. We are bonded by blood. Call any time, any day, with good news or bad. I'm on your side.
Keep an open mind to new ideas and people with different views. Study hard. Laugh often. Keep your honor.
With admiration, respect, and deep love,

Dad (aka Big Guy)

When Luke finished reading the letter, he put it back in the envelope. I reached out to take it back, but he said, "No, no, that's mine now."

The next few days were very difficult. There were many times when I just wanted to pick up the phone and call him, but I didn't want to embarrass him with his new friends or burden him with my loneliness.

On the phone, Big Russ could hear in my voice that I wasn't myself.

"What's wrong?" he asked.

"I miss Luke so much."

"You know, it's just as tough on him," Dad told me.

"Are you kidding? He's having the time of his life."

That's what I thought, but a year later, Luke told me that Big Russ had been right. "That first semester was really tough," he said. "But I knew I couldn't say anything because you would have wanted to come up, and that wouldn't have been good for either of us."

The wisdom of my father, spoken by my son.

Acknowledgments

Once again, Bill Novak was my full partner in writing and assembling this book. He is organized, disciplined, and gifted—and he is also a wonderful father.

Susan Mercandetti brought me to Random House. Her confidence, encouragement, and keen editor's eye were invaluable. Associate editor Jonathan Jao was tireless and precise. The entire Random House organization was just superb.

Bob Barnett offered wise counsel and sound advice. He is a terrific lawyer and loyal friend.

My NBC colleagues, especially the Washington bureau managers—Wendy Wilkinson, Brady Daniels, Larry Gaetano, and Rachel Manning—were endlessly supportive. The **Meet the Press** team, with the indomitable Betsy Fischer along with Michelle Jaconi, Chris Donovan, Ted Kresse, Ellen Van de Mark, Rebecca Samuels, Leigh Sutherland, and the entire crew were extraordinary with their preparation and dedication. Senior Producer Barbara Fant planned, arranged, and oversaw my CNBC tapings with precision and ingenuity. Lisa Havlovitz and Michelle Perry ran my office with efficiency and aplomb, allowing me to do my job **and** work on this book.

My wife, Maureen, my son, Luke, Buster the Wonder Dog, and my sisters B.A., Kiki, and Trish were there as always—and do they keep me grounded!

A very special thank-you to the more than sixty thousand of you who sent such heartfelt letters and e-mails about your own dads. I wish I could publish them all.

Wisdom of Our Fathers
P.O. Box 5999
Washington, DC 20016

www.wisdomofourfathers.com